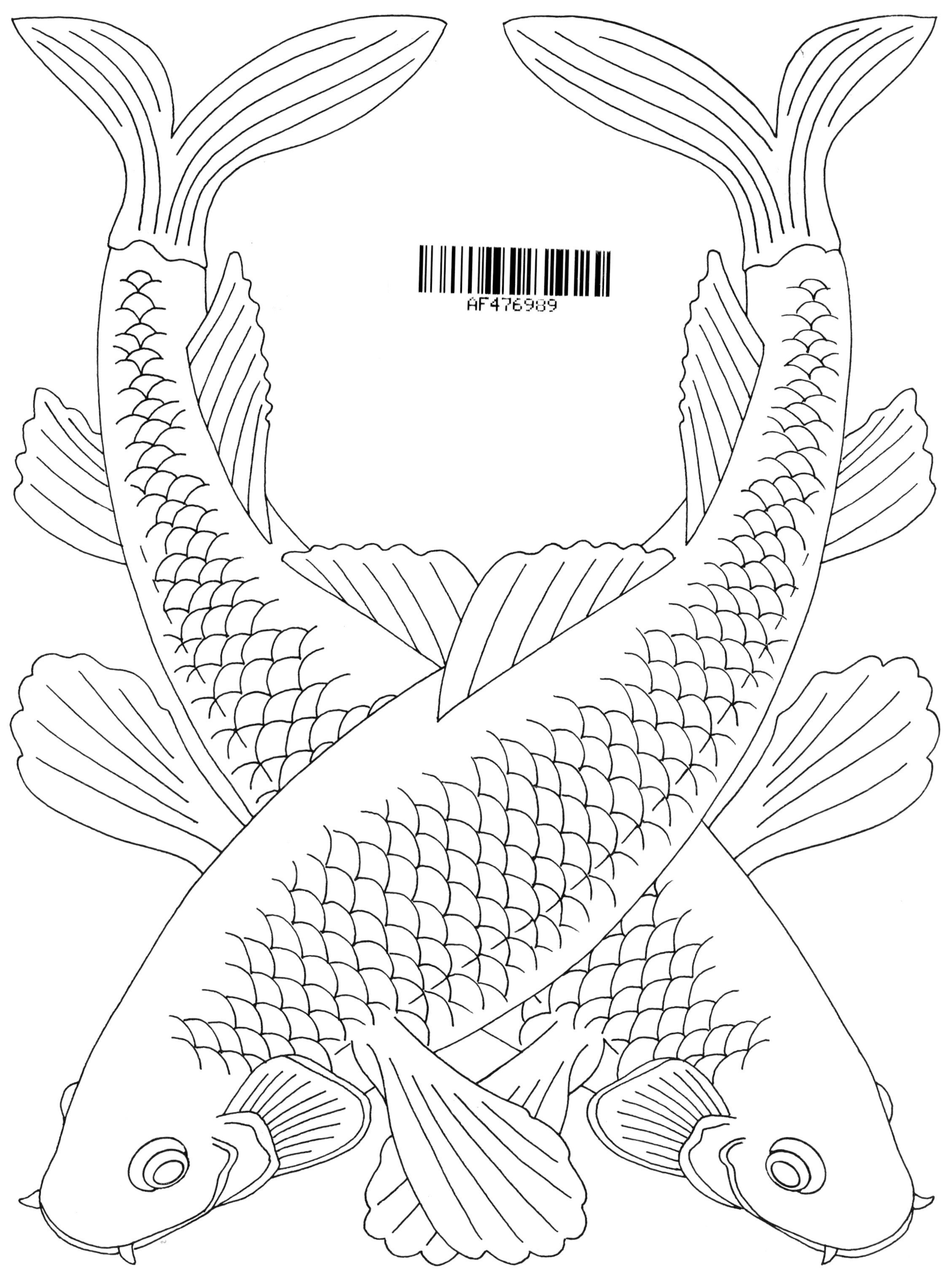
AF476989

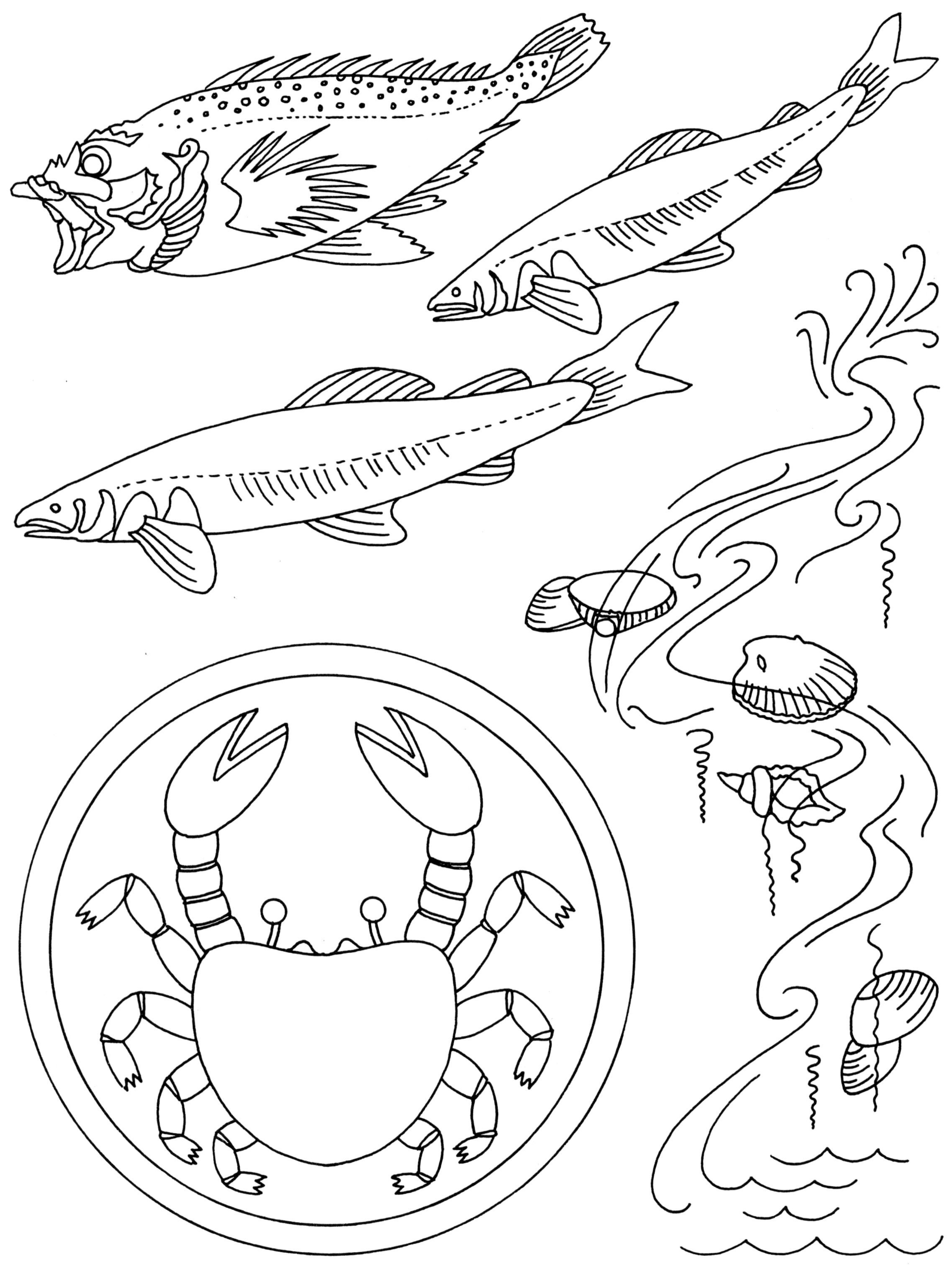

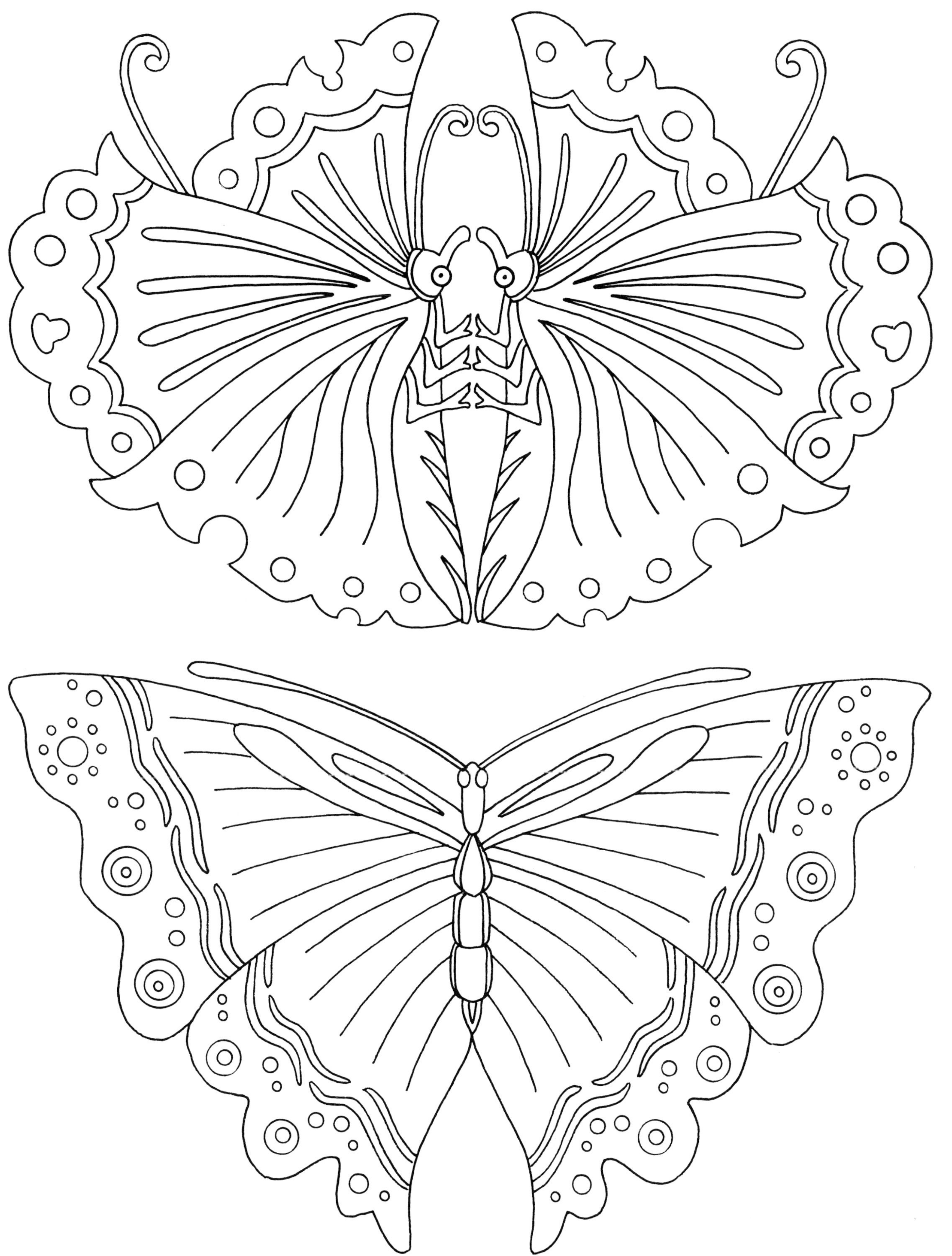

Butterflies

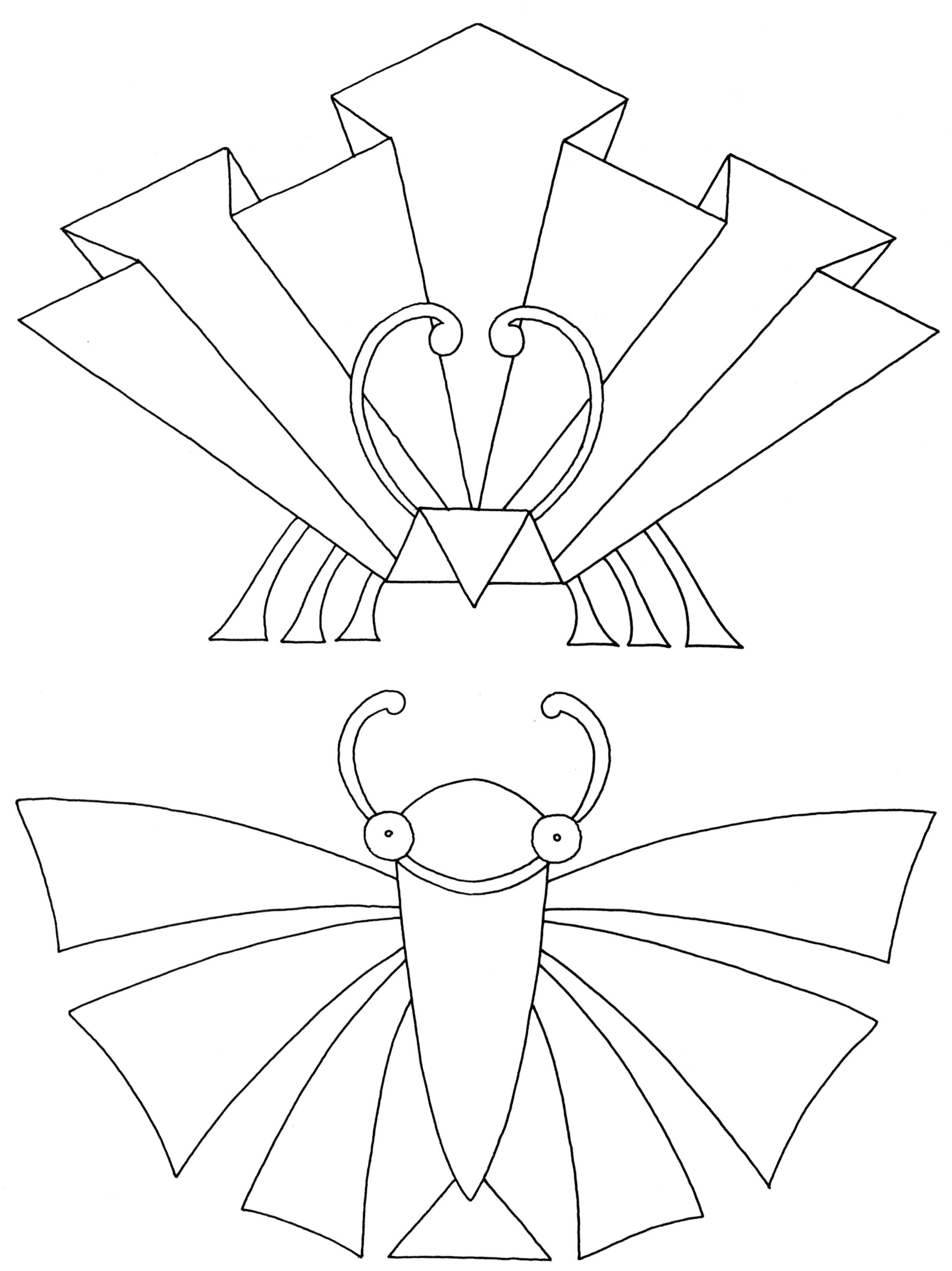

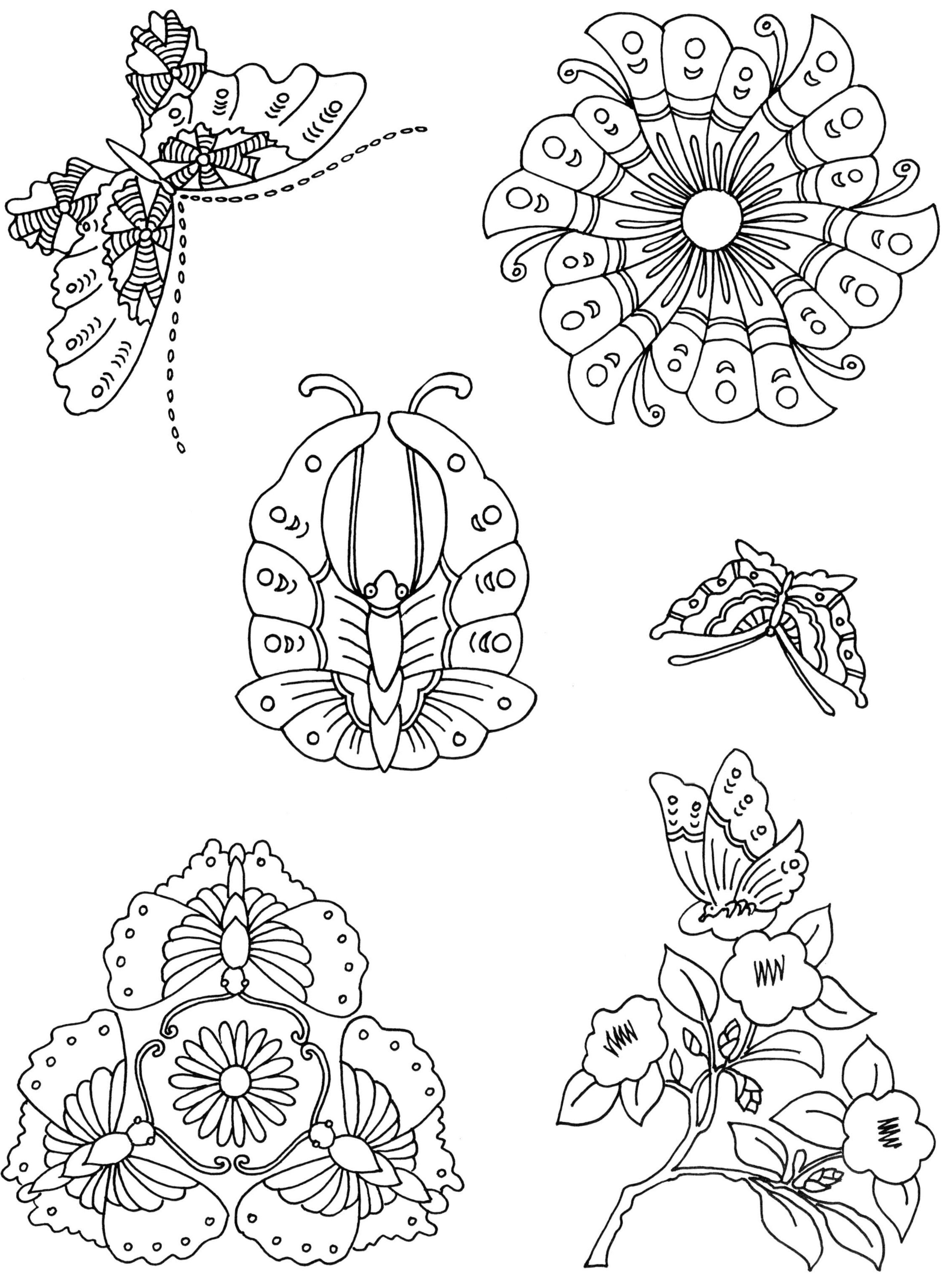

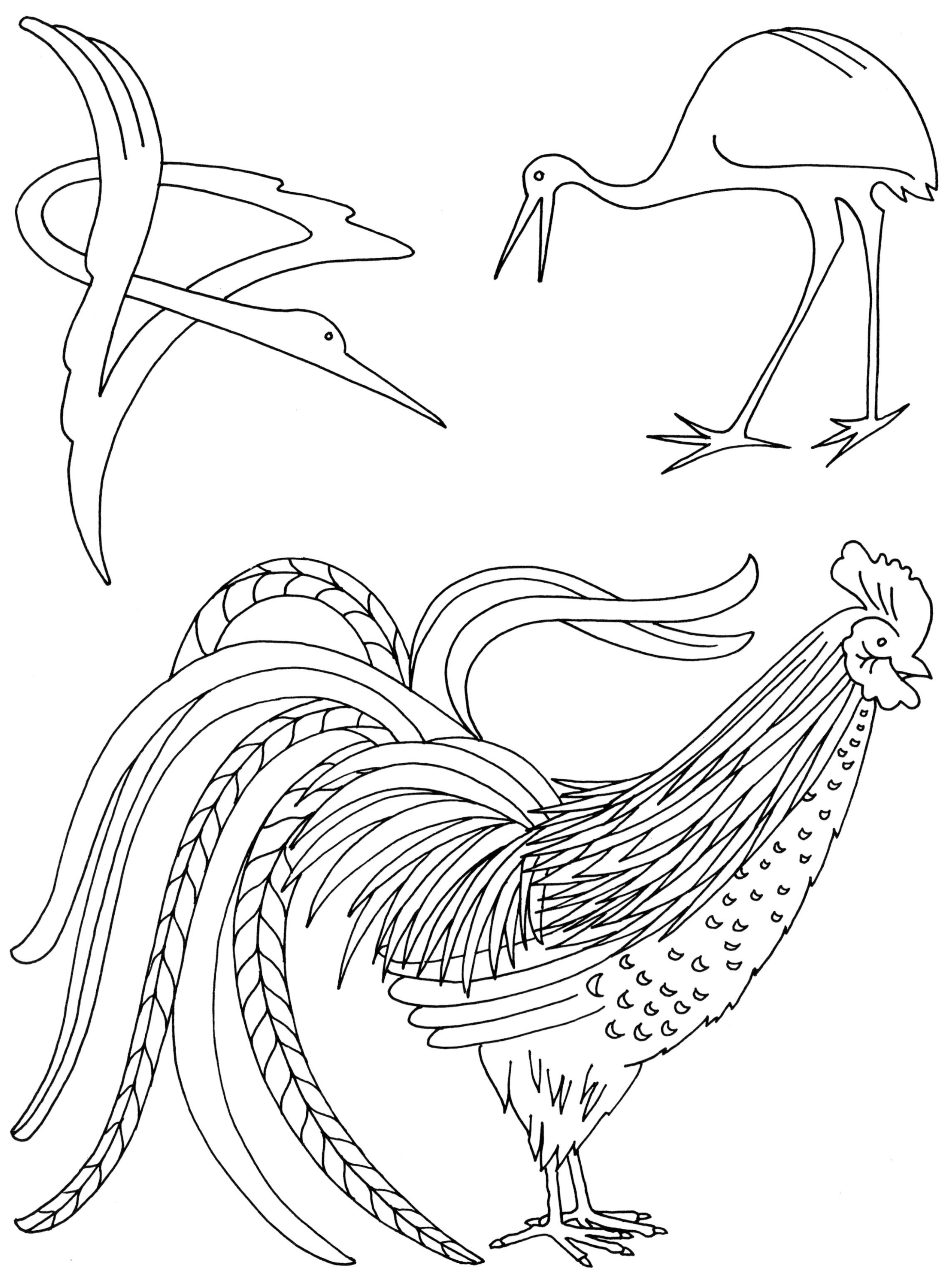

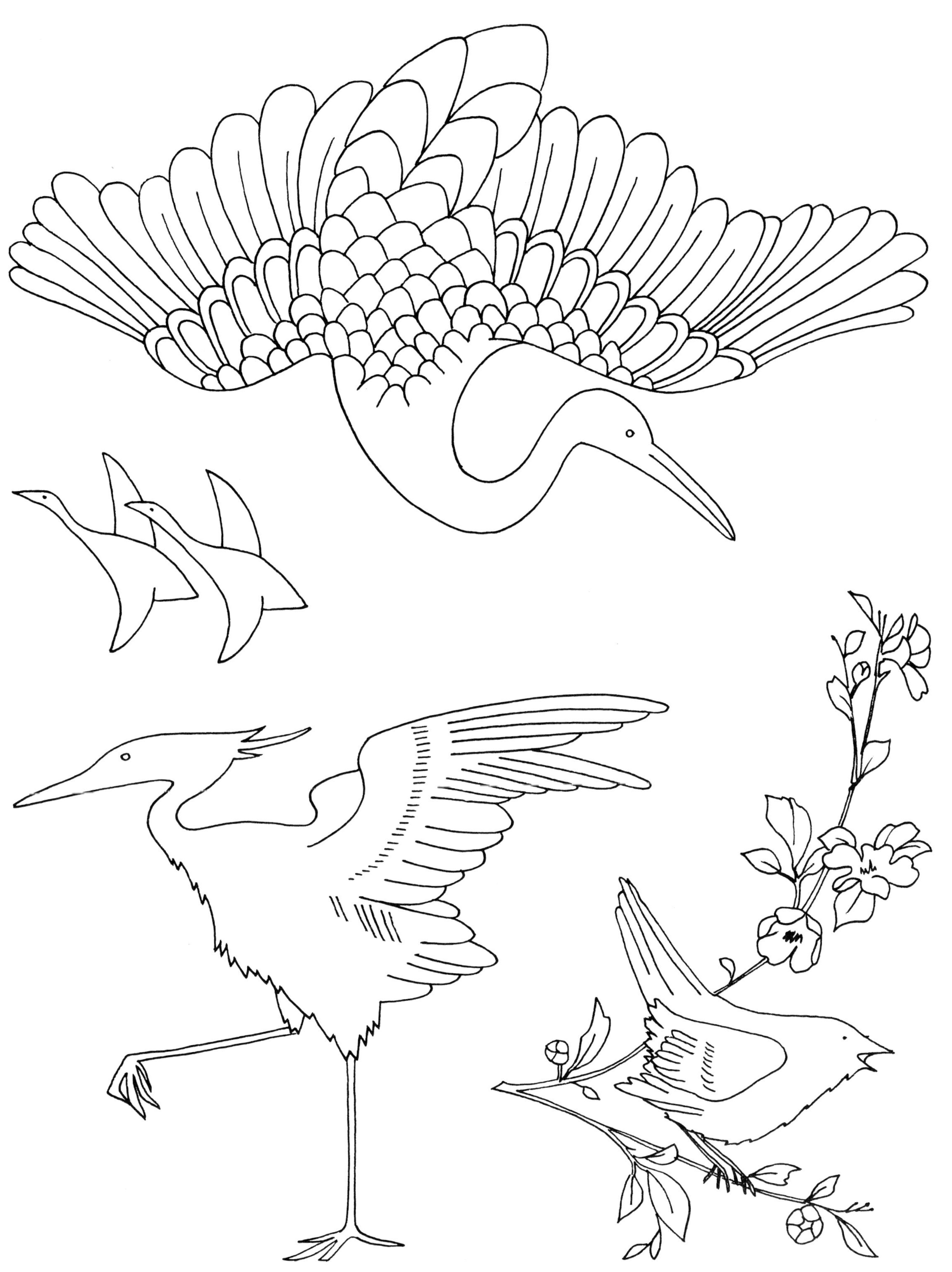

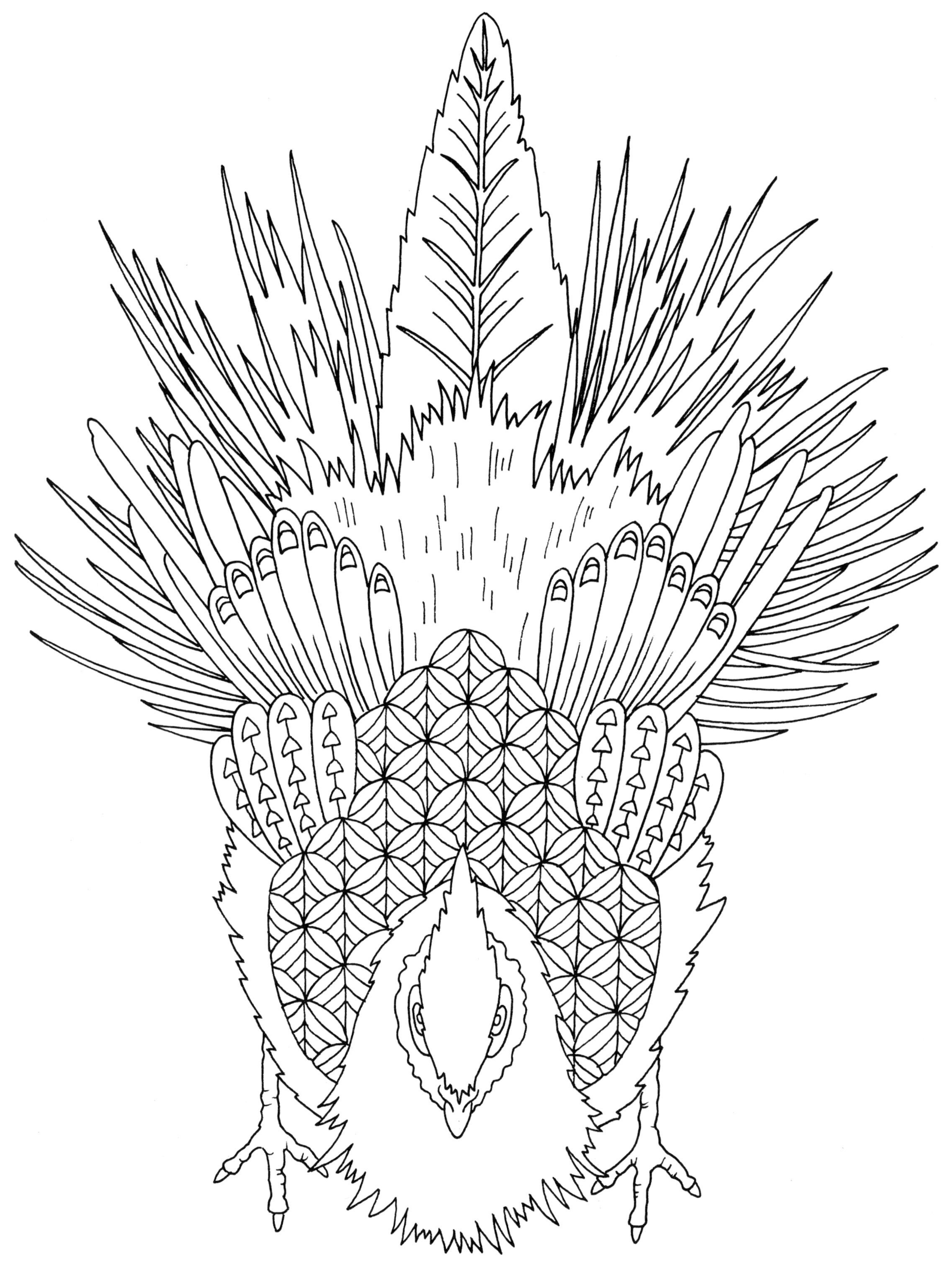

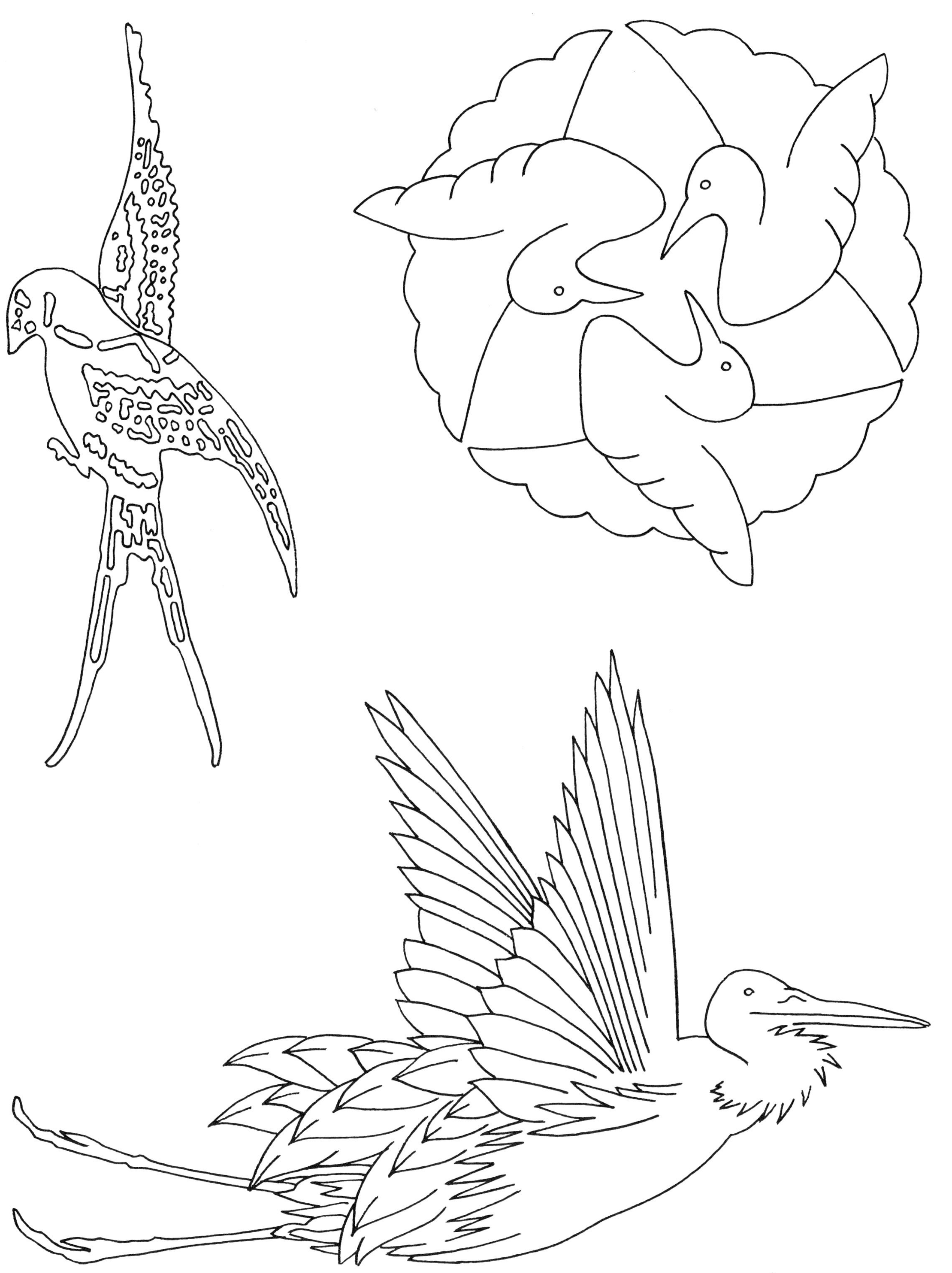

Waves

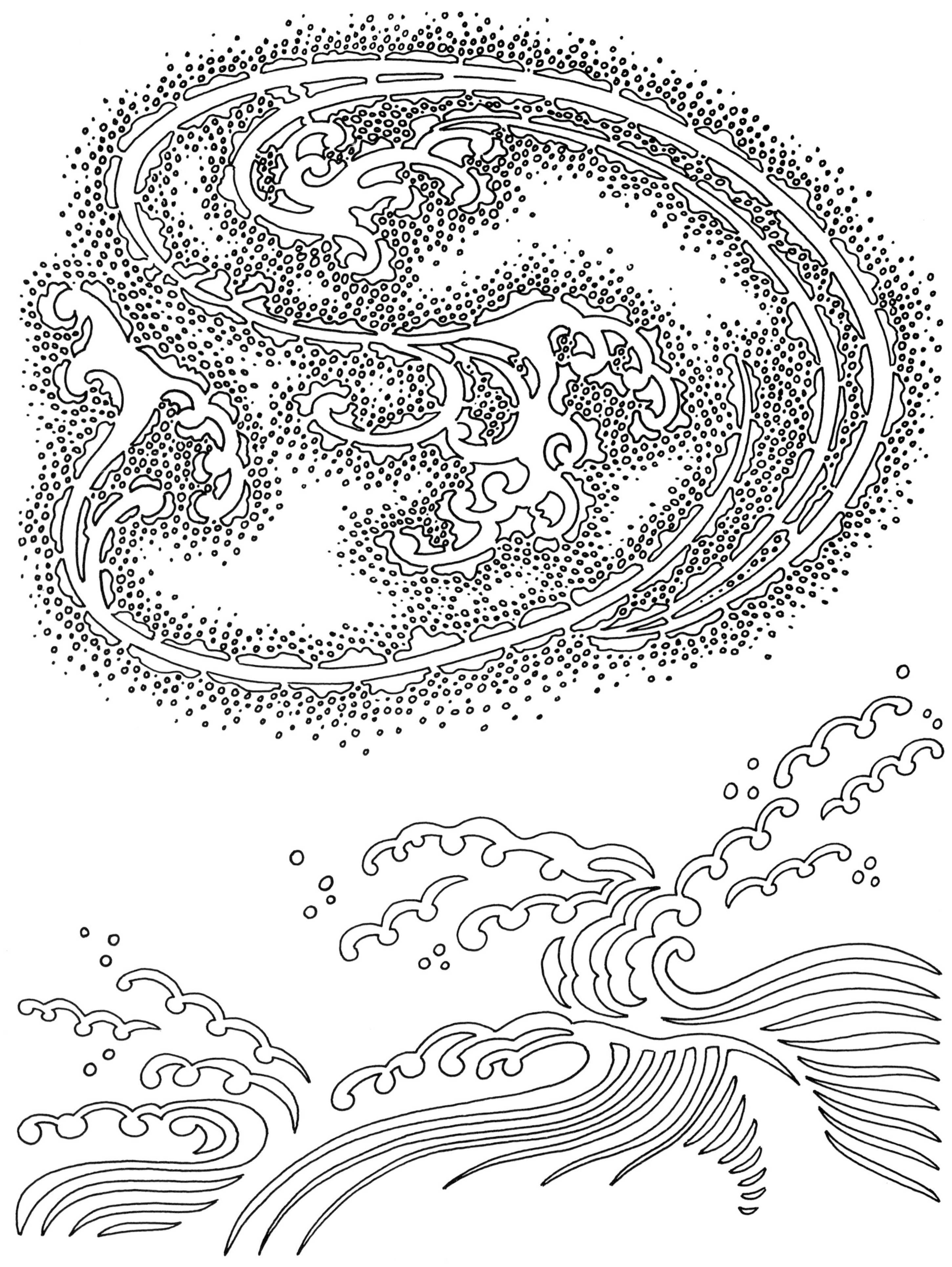

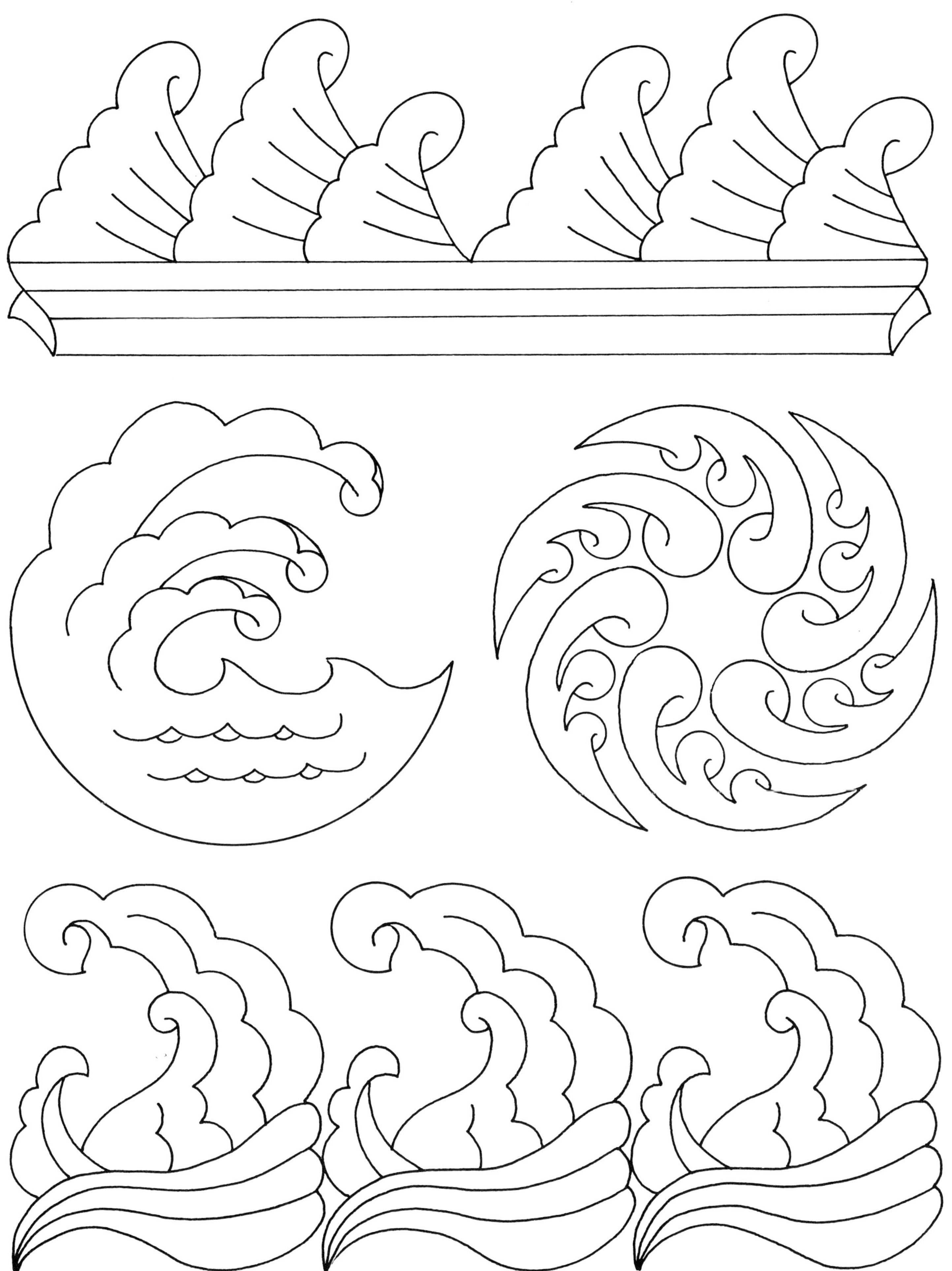

Waves

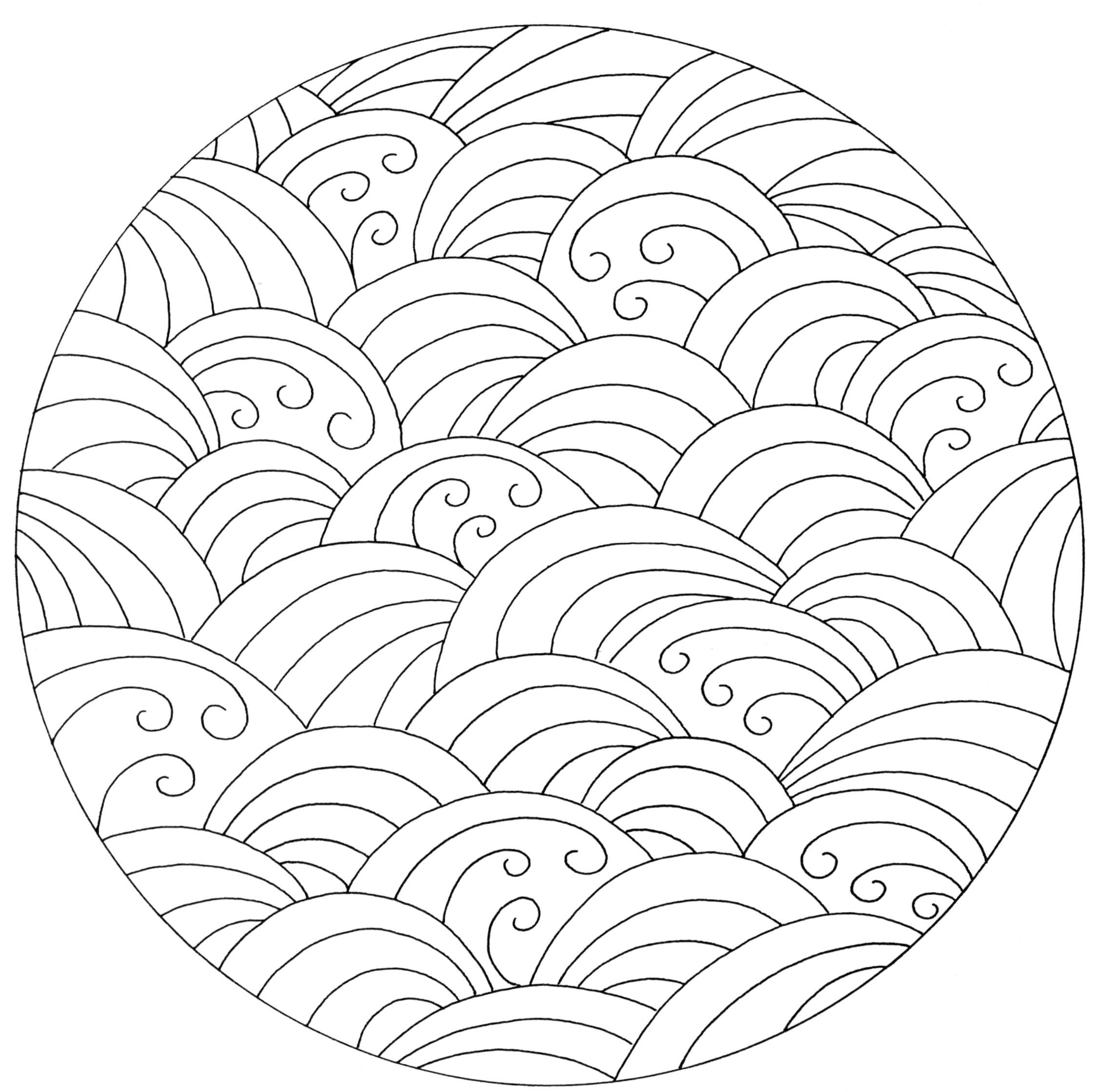

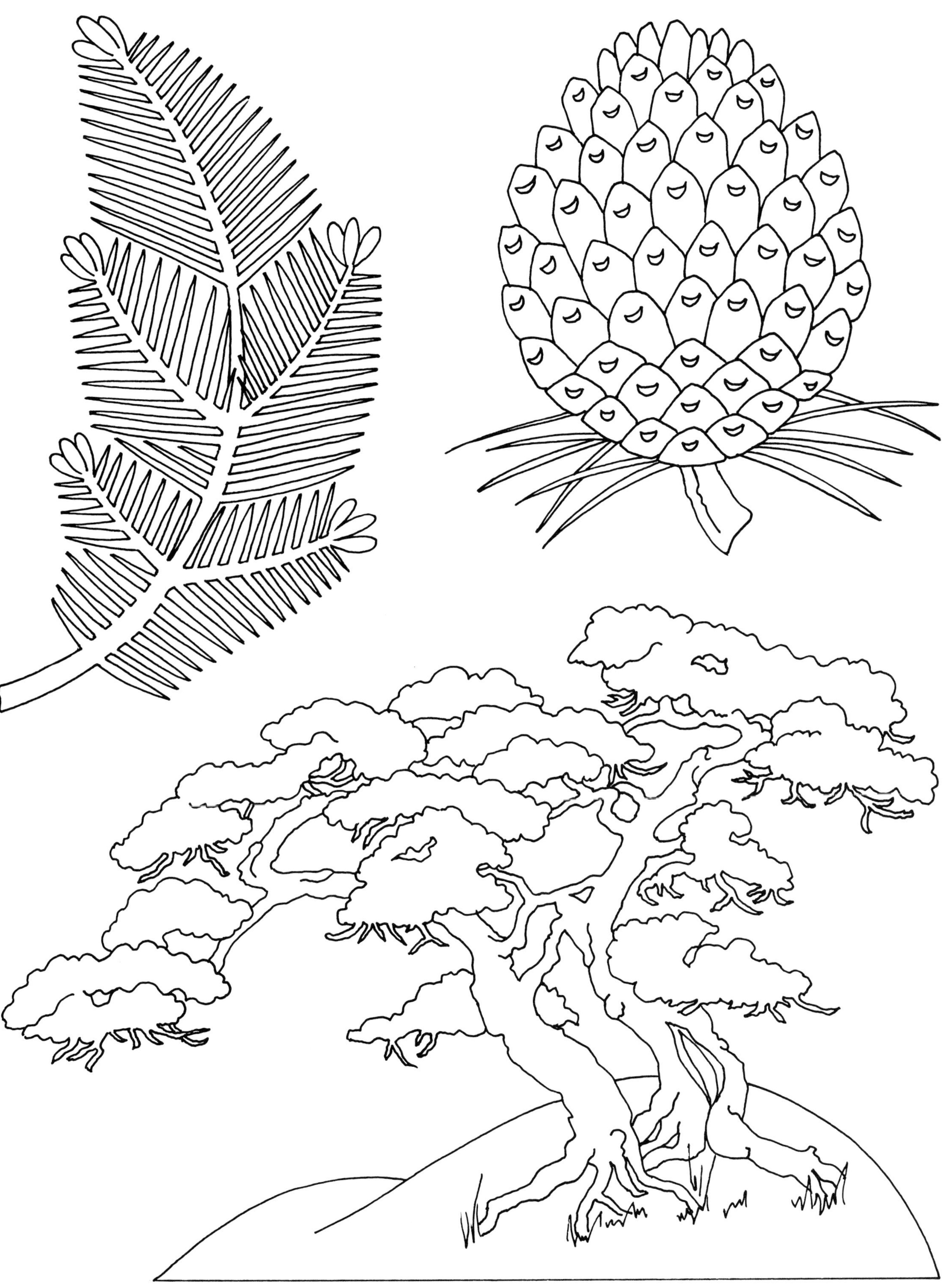

Bamboo

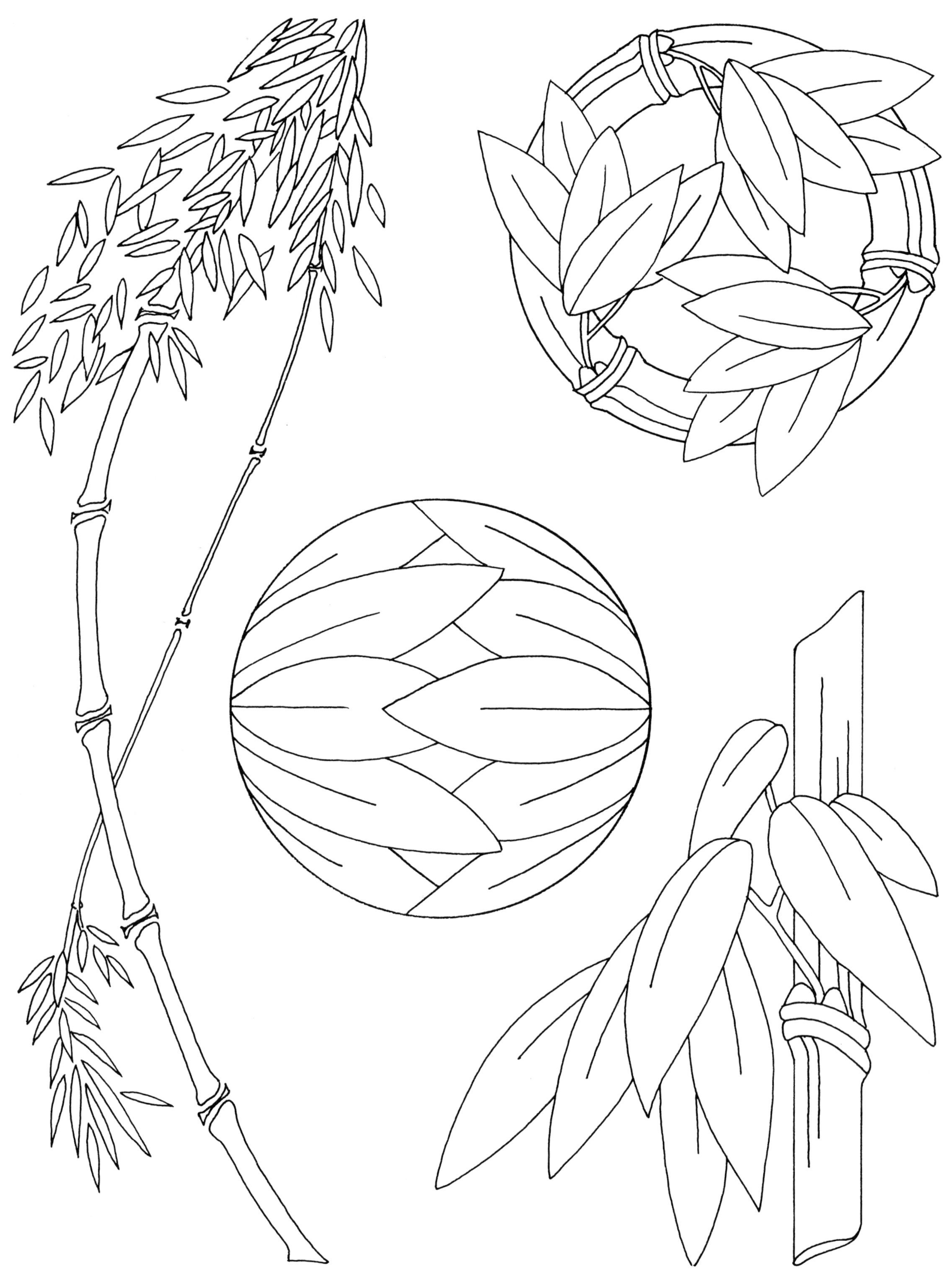

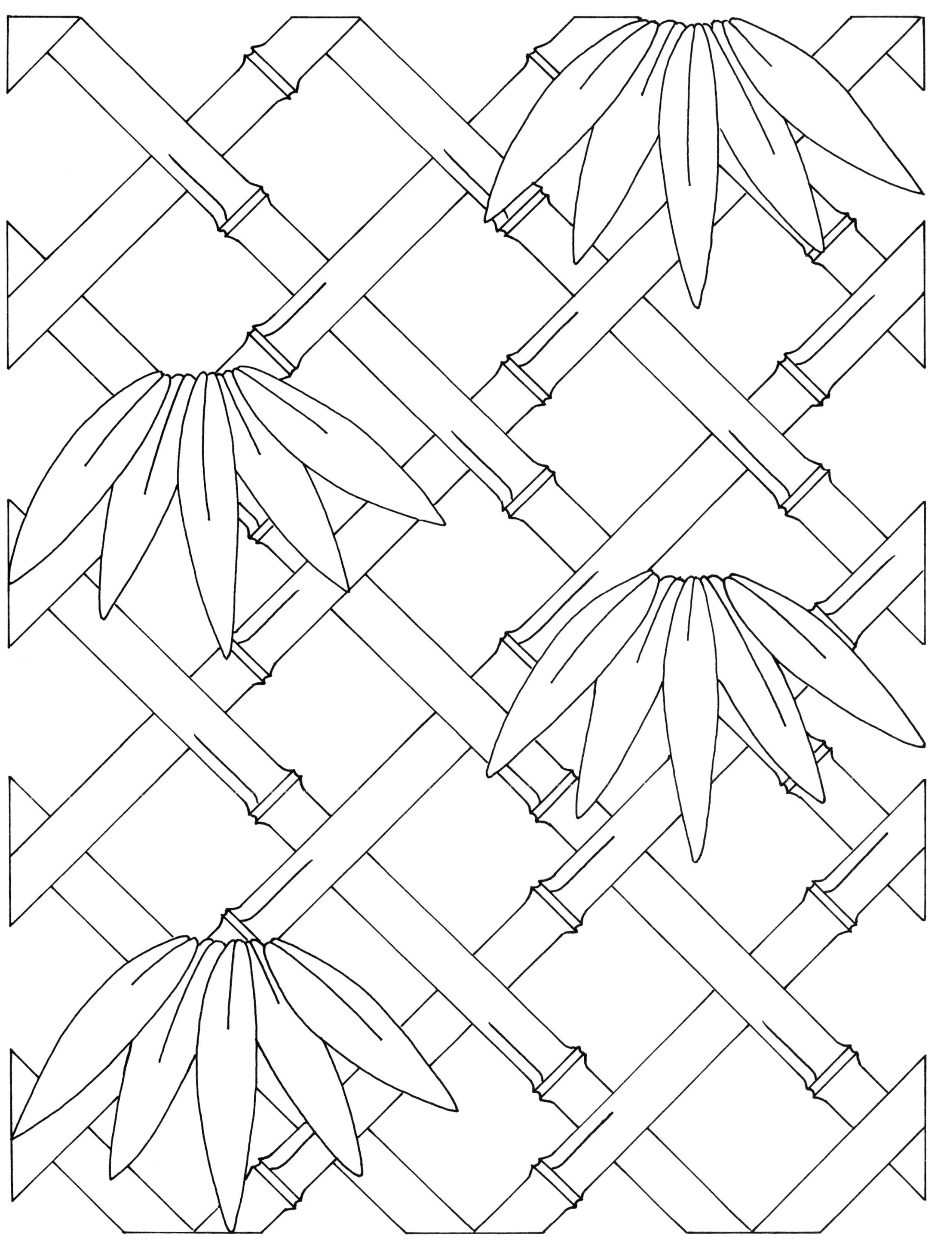

Blossom

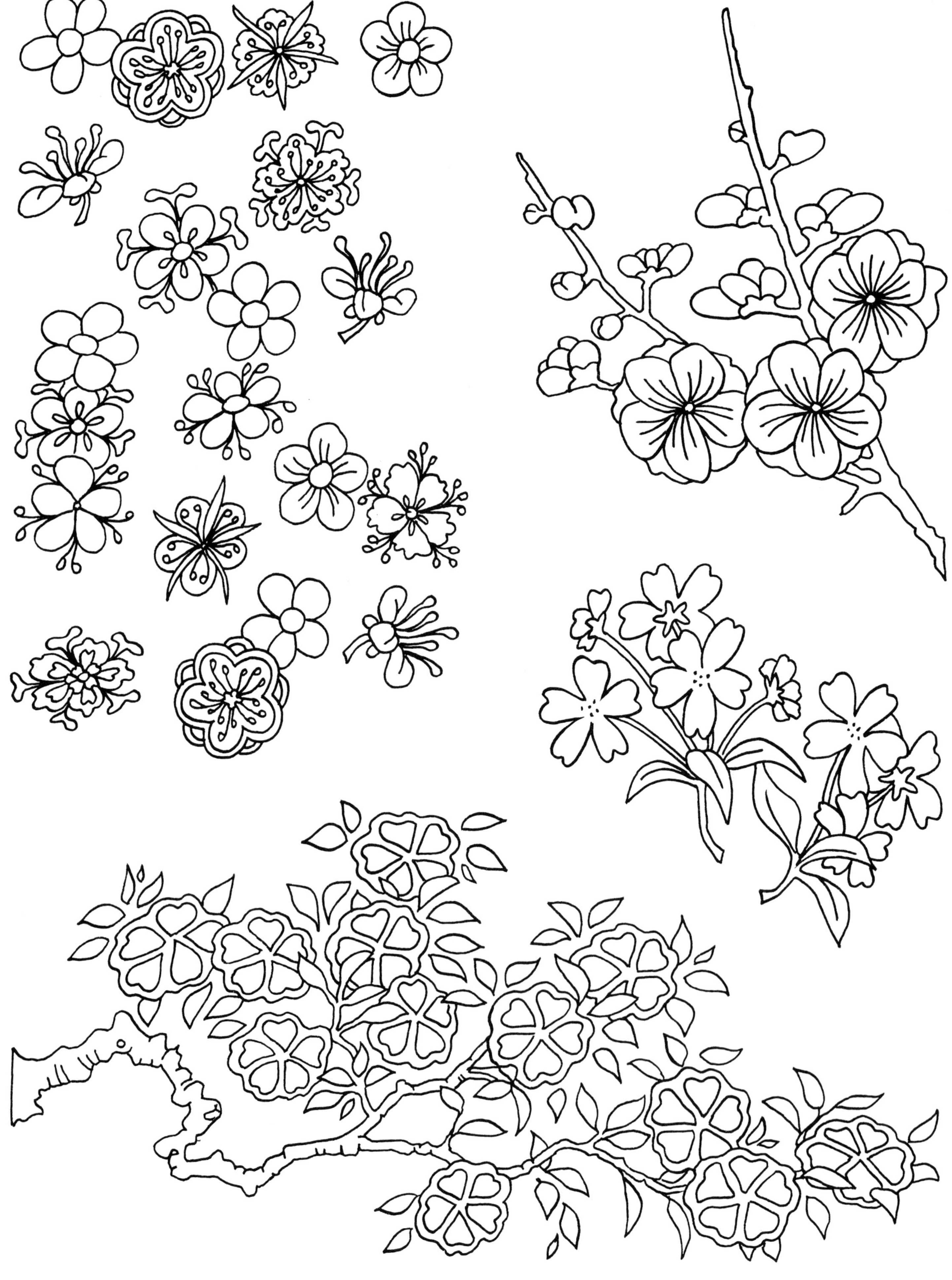

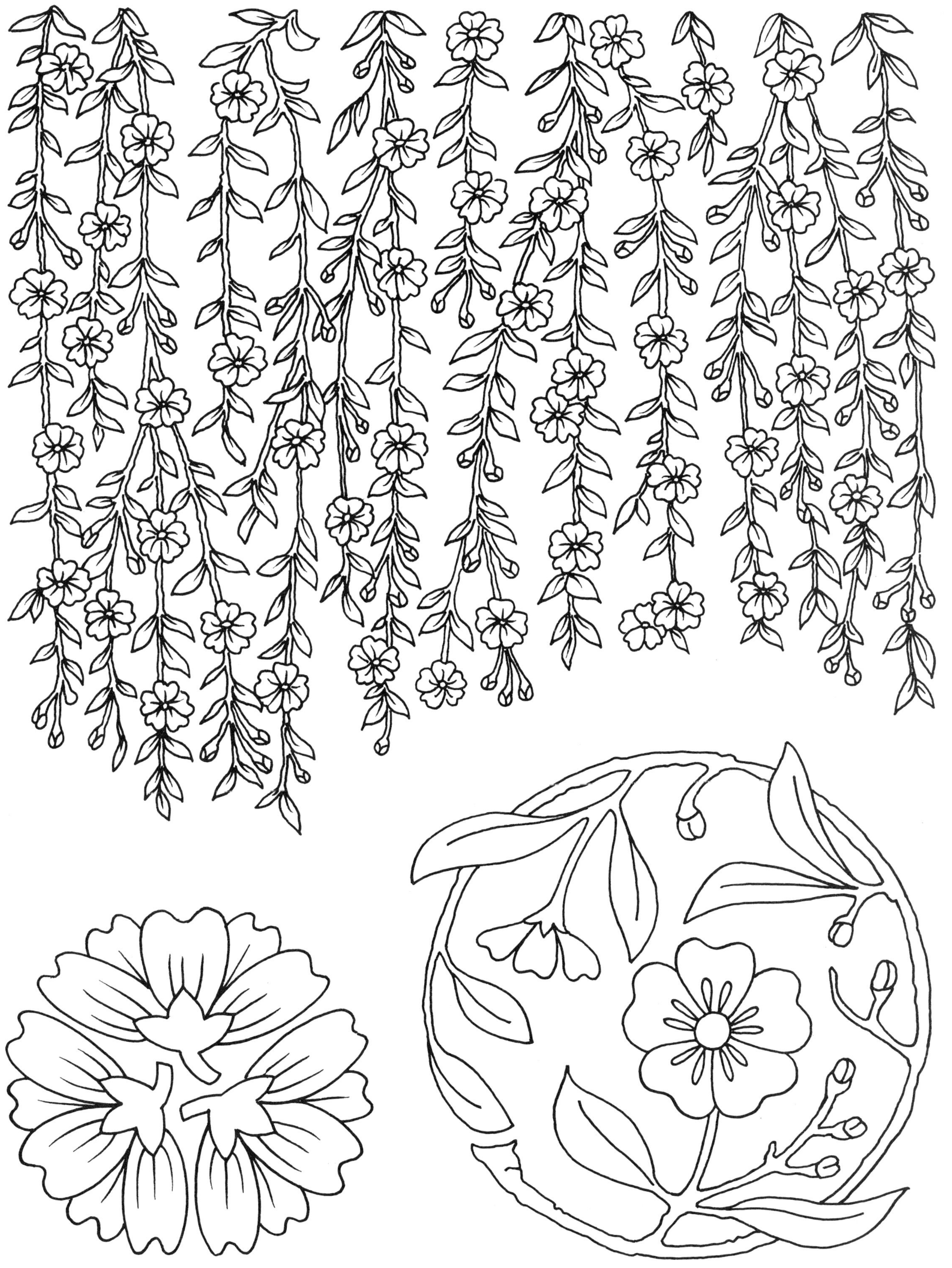

Blossom

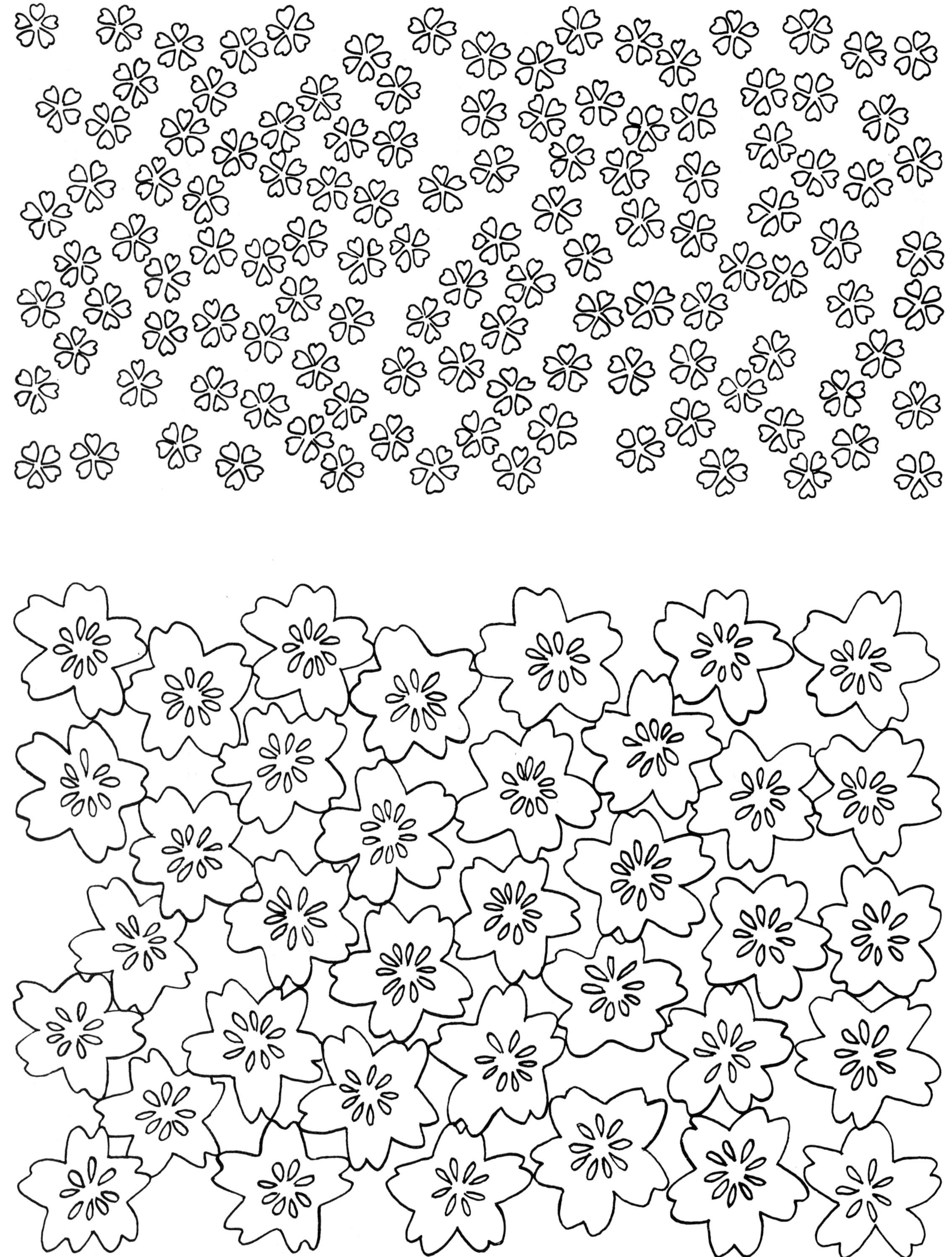

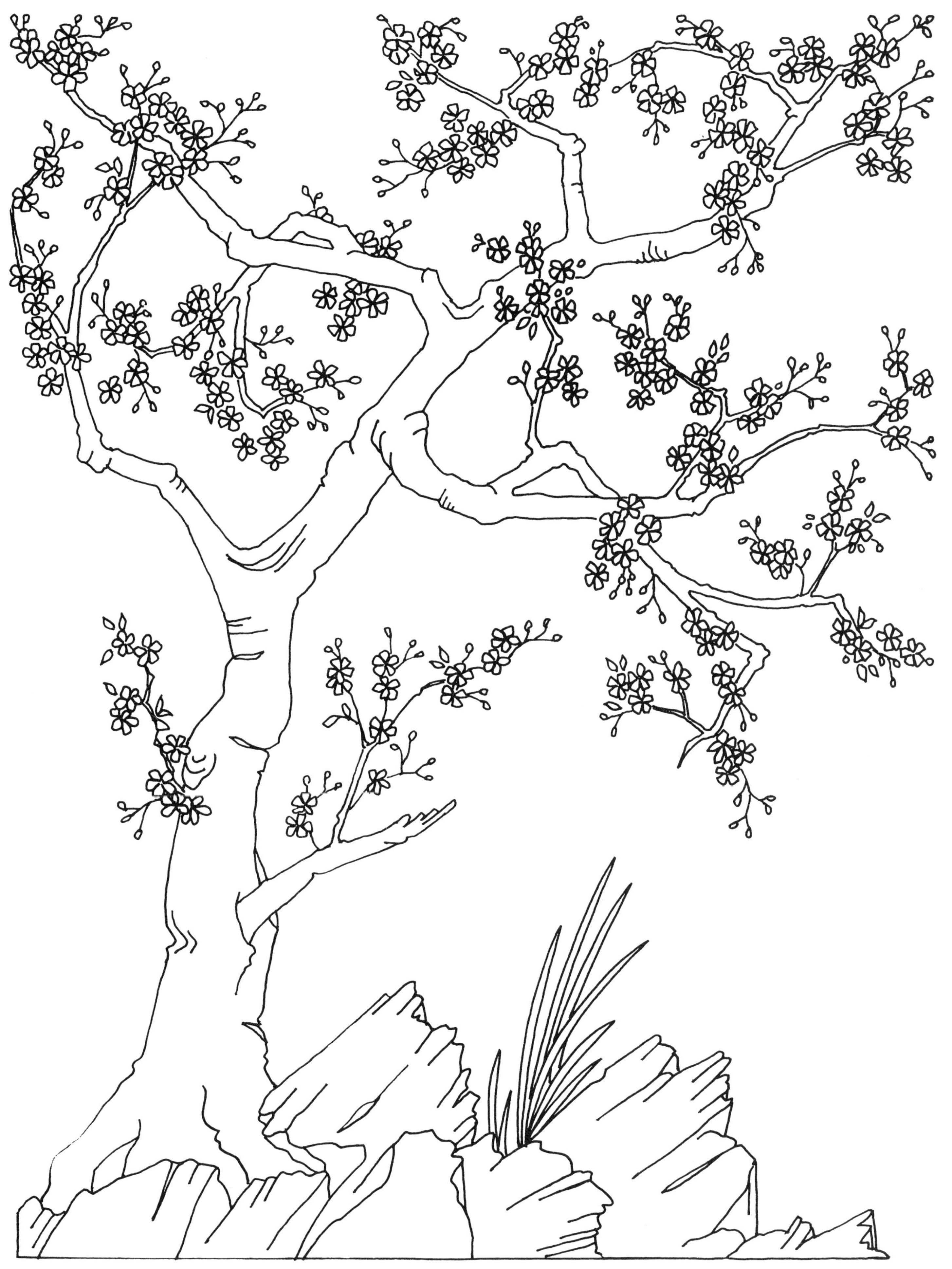

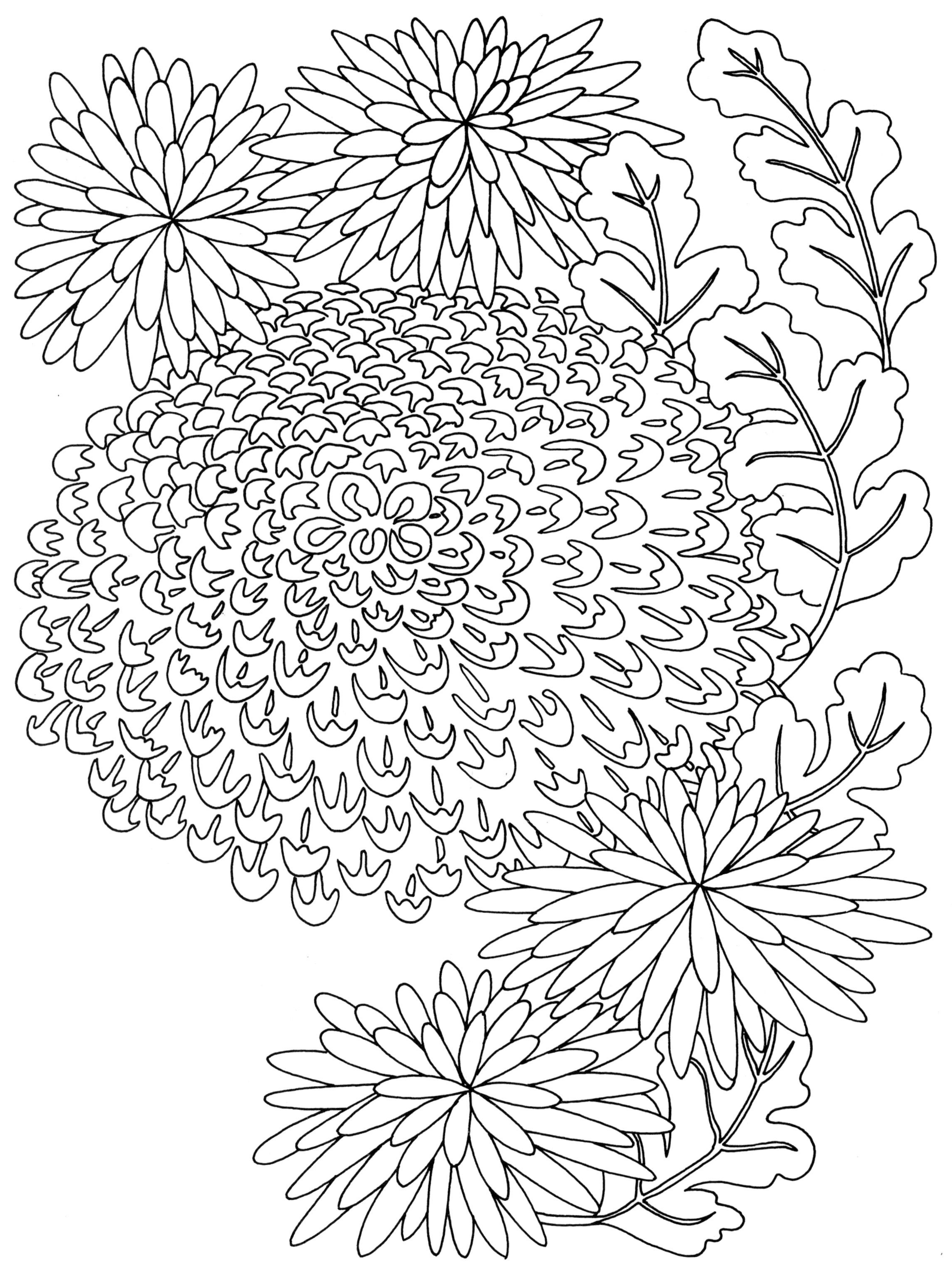

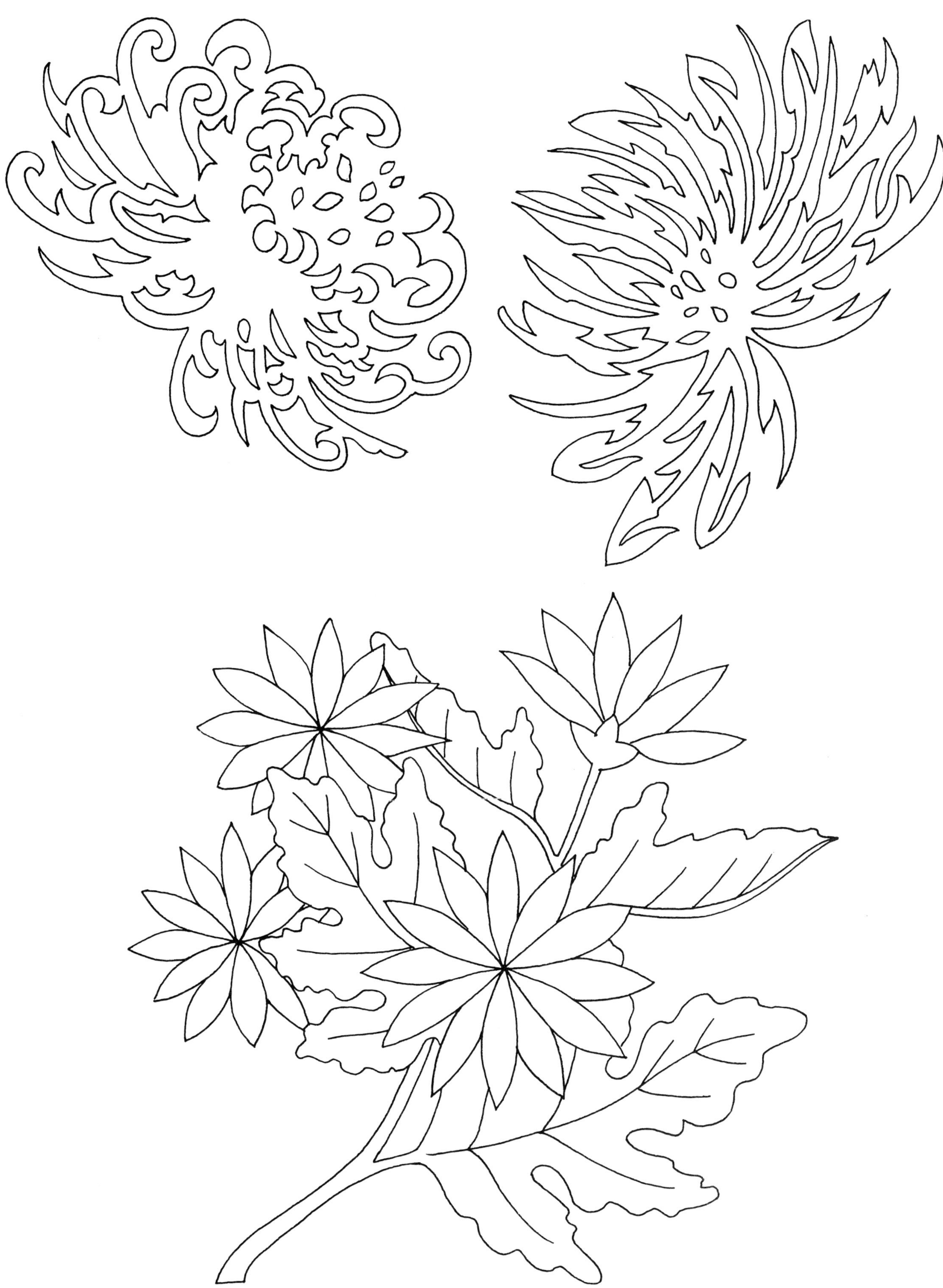

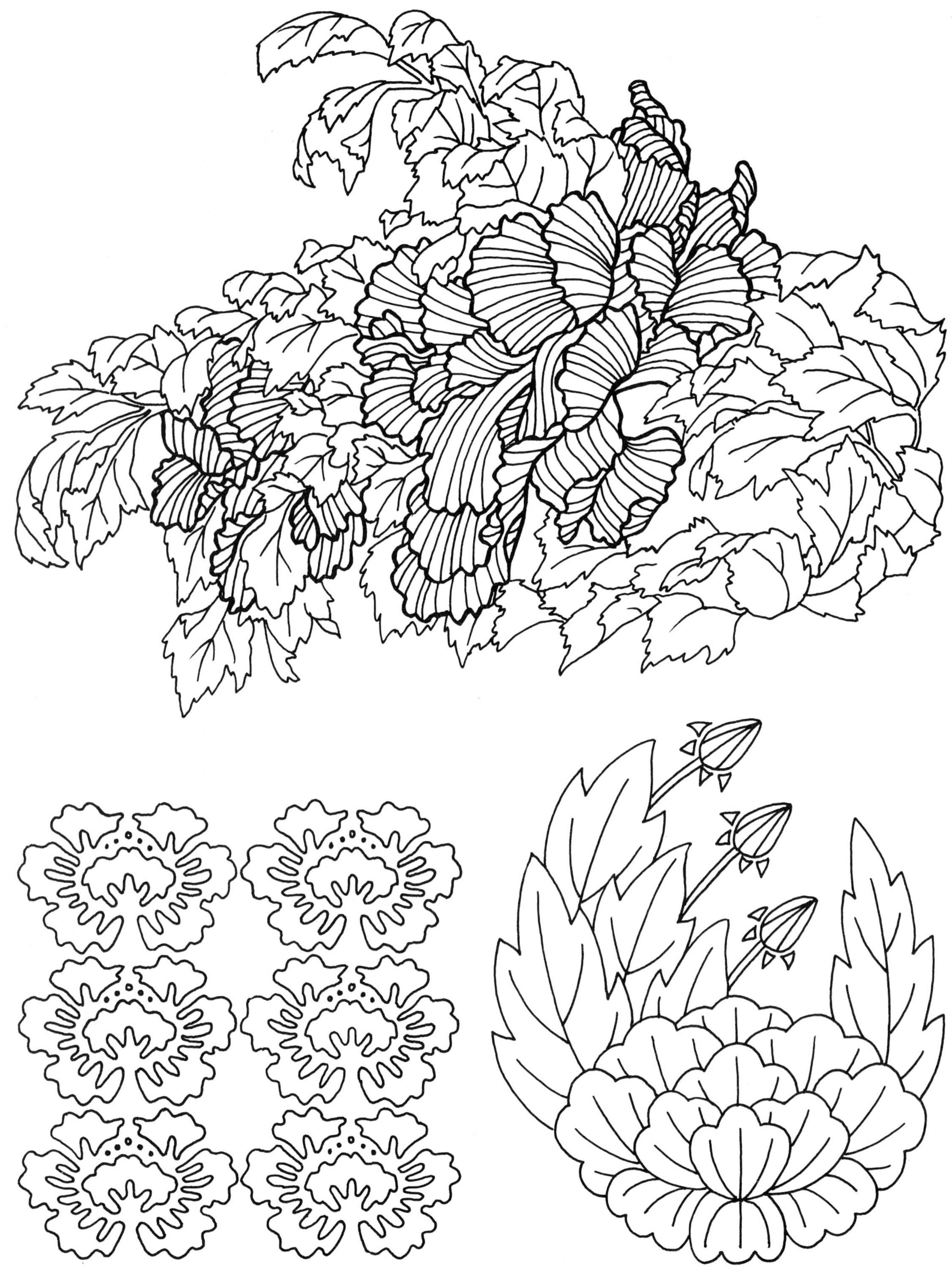

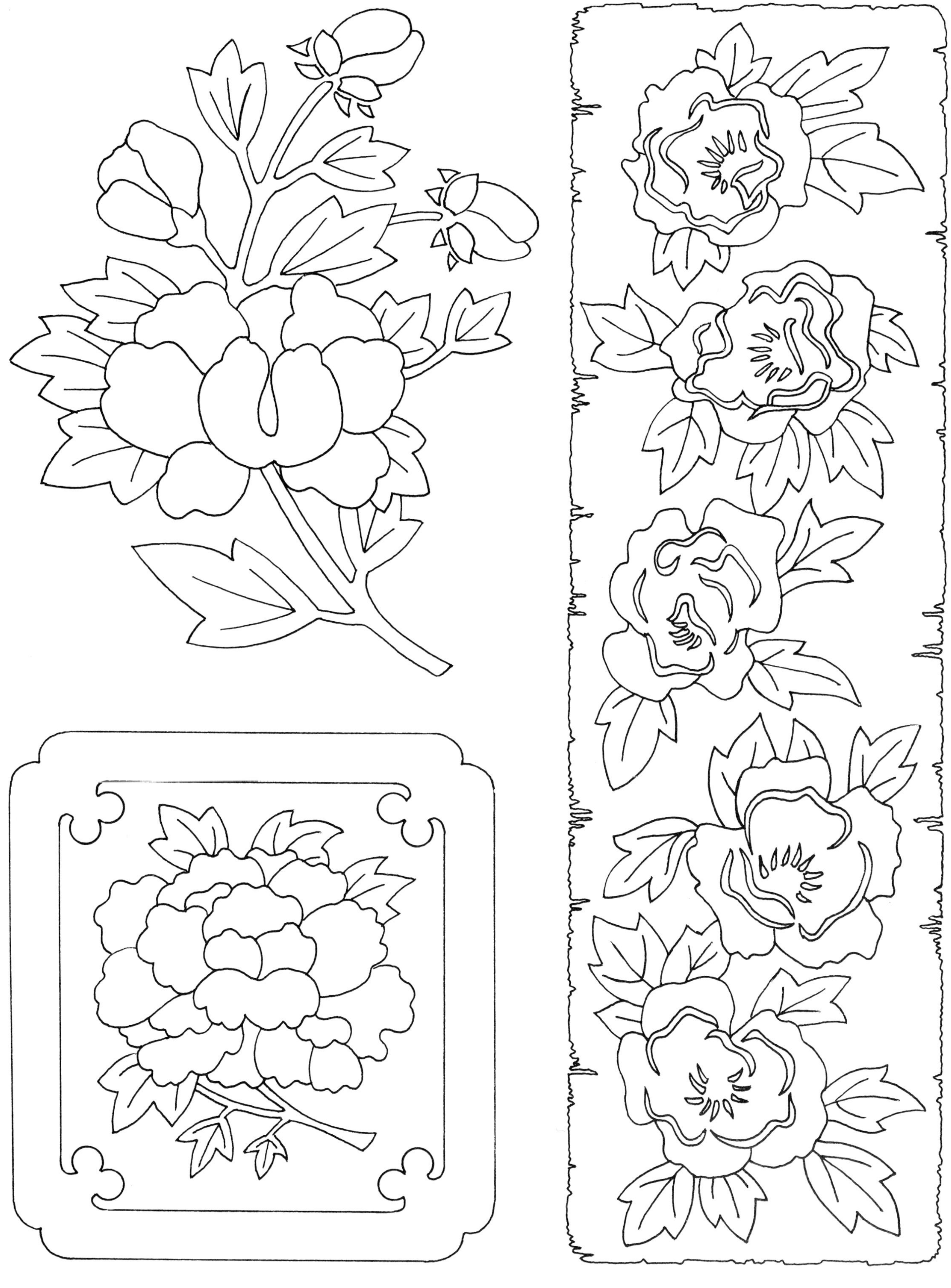

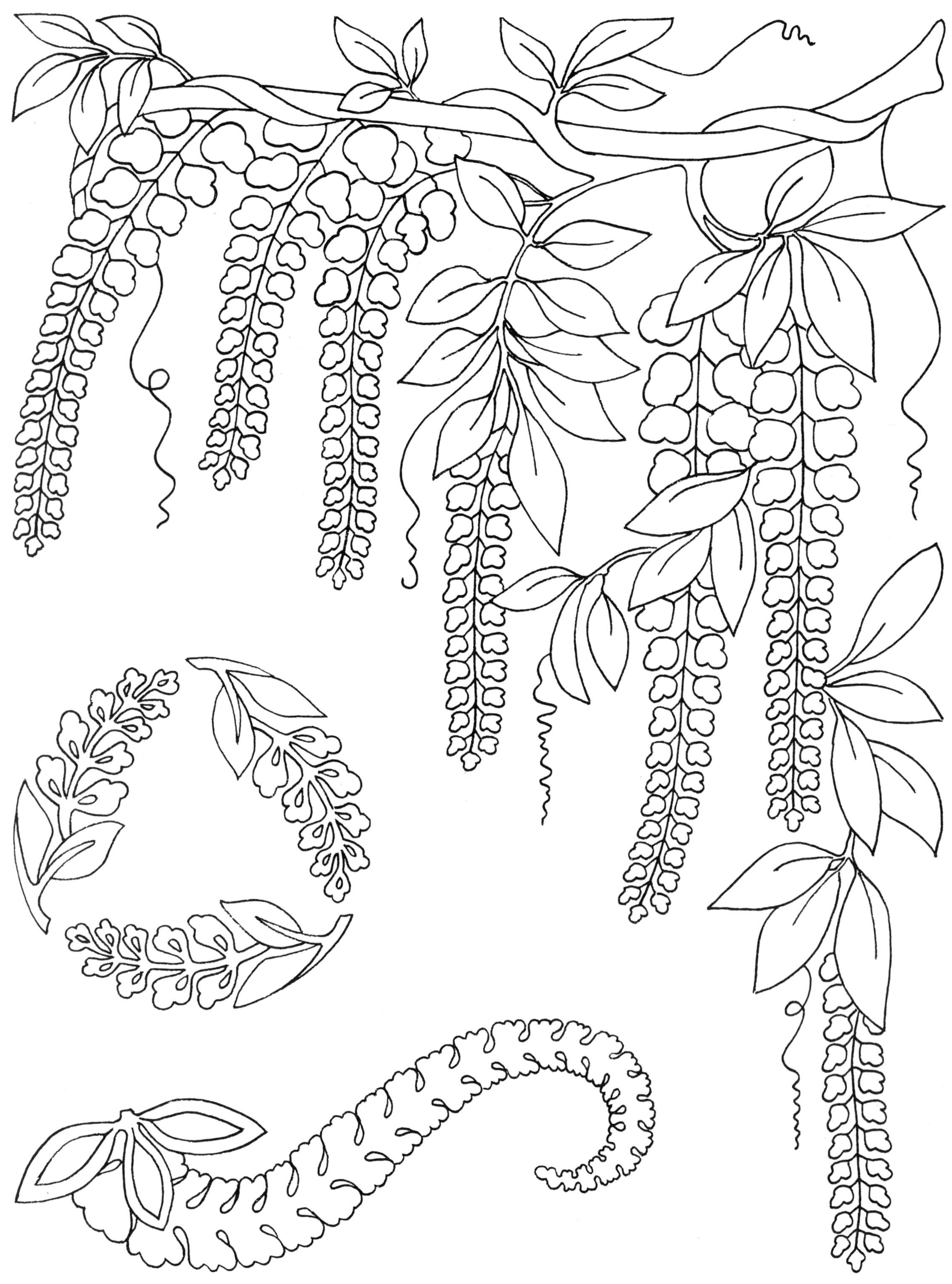

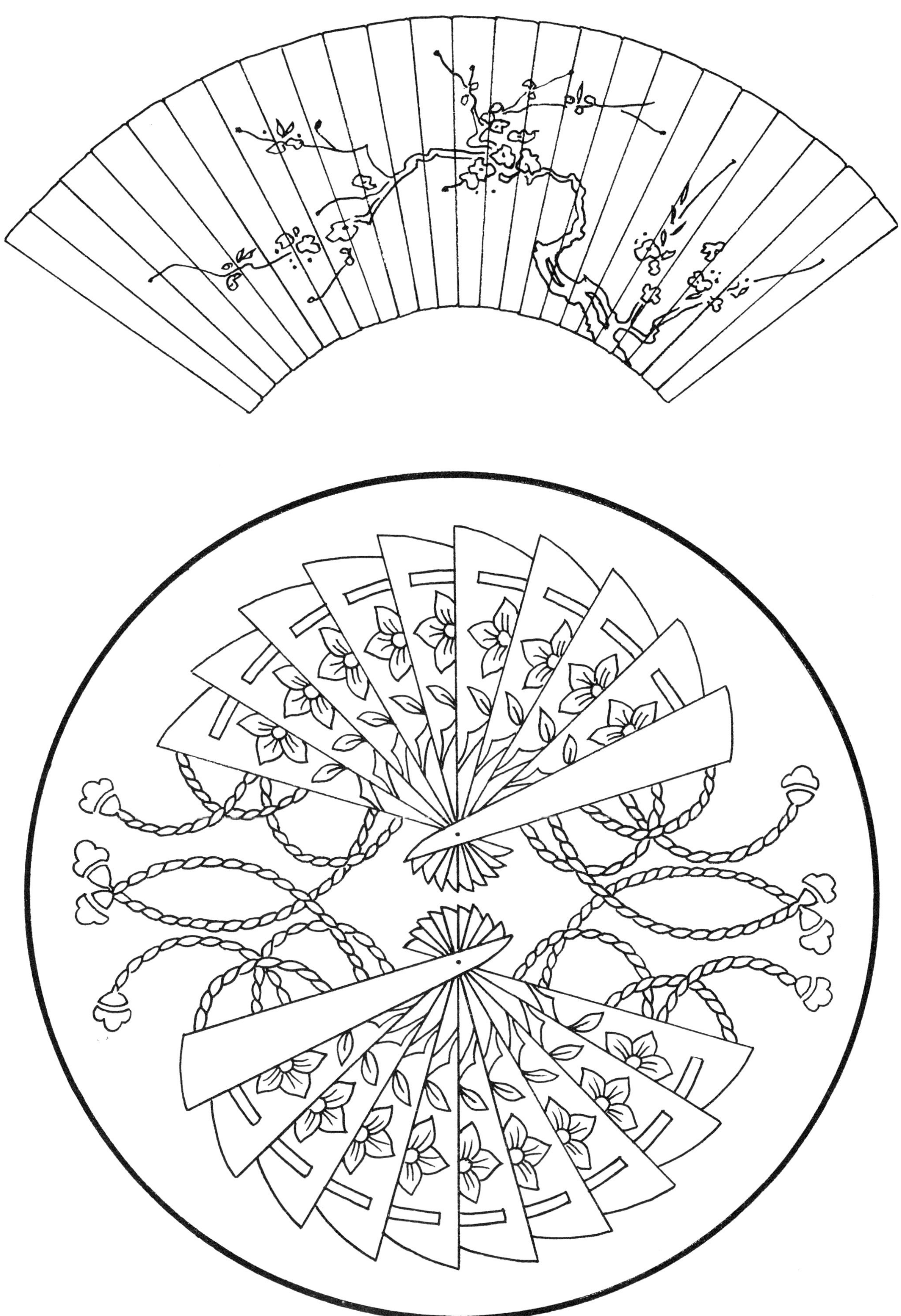

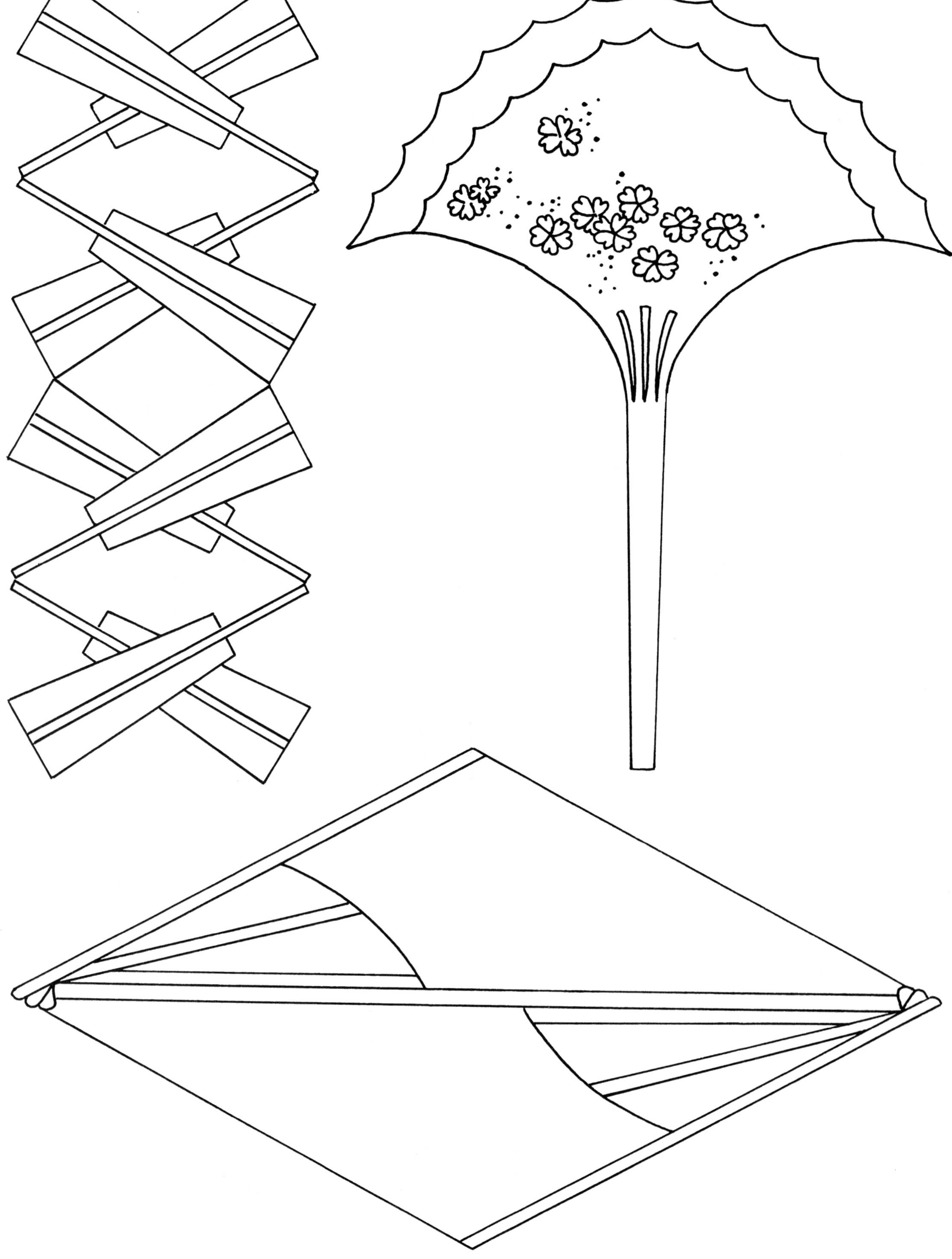

SEARCH PRESS LIMITED

independent book publishers since 1970

AFFIX
STAMP
HERE

Search Press Ltd
Wellwood, North Farm Road
Tunbridge Wells
Kent
TN2 3DR
United Kingdom

We hope you enjoy using this book as much as we enjoyed preparing it for you. Other Search Press books are available from all good art and craft outlets and bookshops. If you wish to be kept informed of new titles, and receive a free colour catalogue, then please fill in your details below and return this card to the address overleaf.

Mr/Mrs/Ms/Miss _________ Initials _________ Surname _________________________

____

____Postcode _______________________

Country_________________________________ Telephone No. _______________________

Title of book in which this card was found: _________________________________

Where purchased: ____

Subject on which you would like to see a book published: ___________________________

Have you ever bought books via the internet?   Yes / No

Your e-mail address (optional): ____

Thank you for taking the time to fill in this card.

For US customers, telephone toll-free on (800) 289-9276, or post this card to: Search Press USA, 1338 Ross Street, Petaluma, CA 94954.

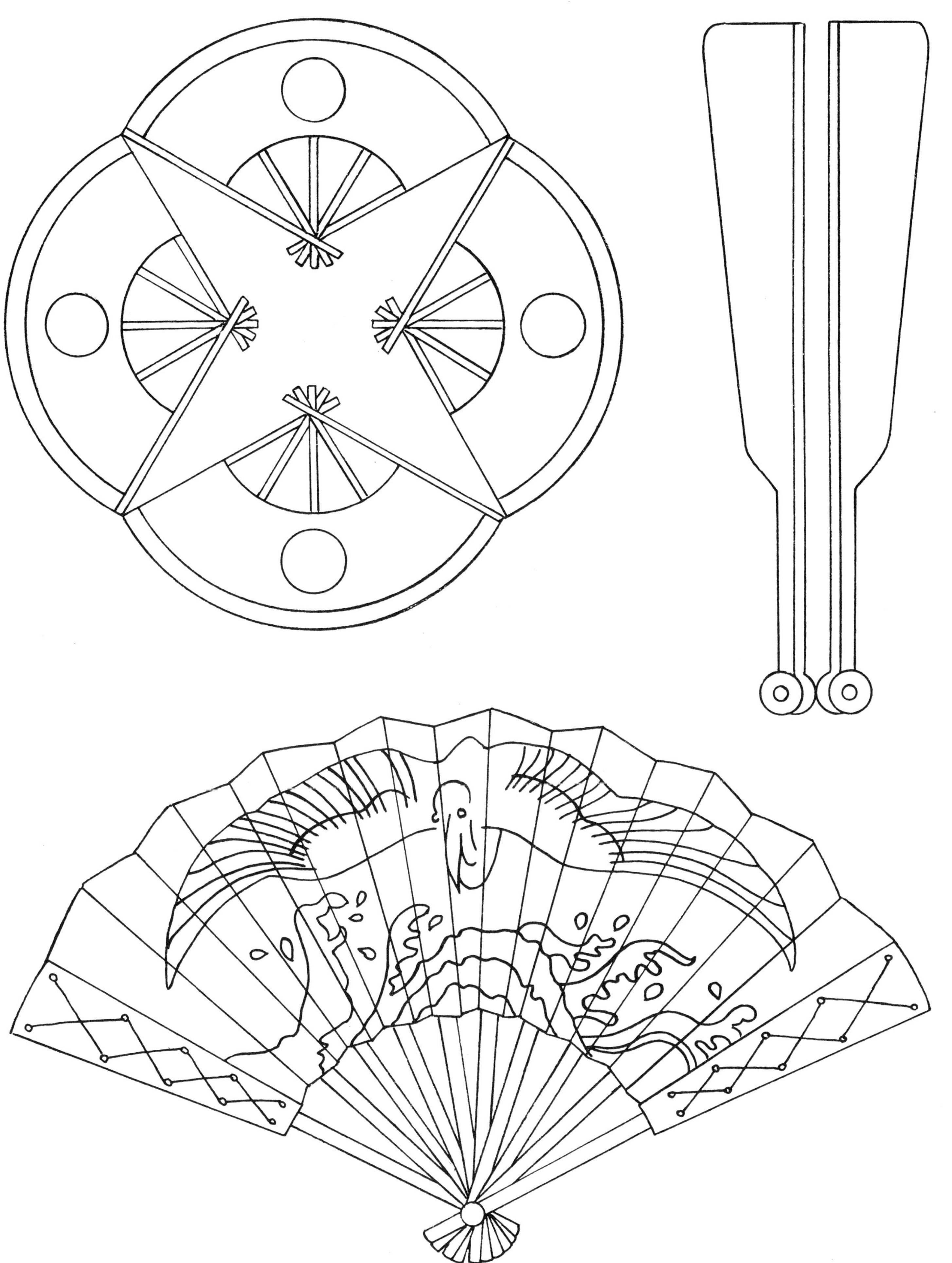

Masks

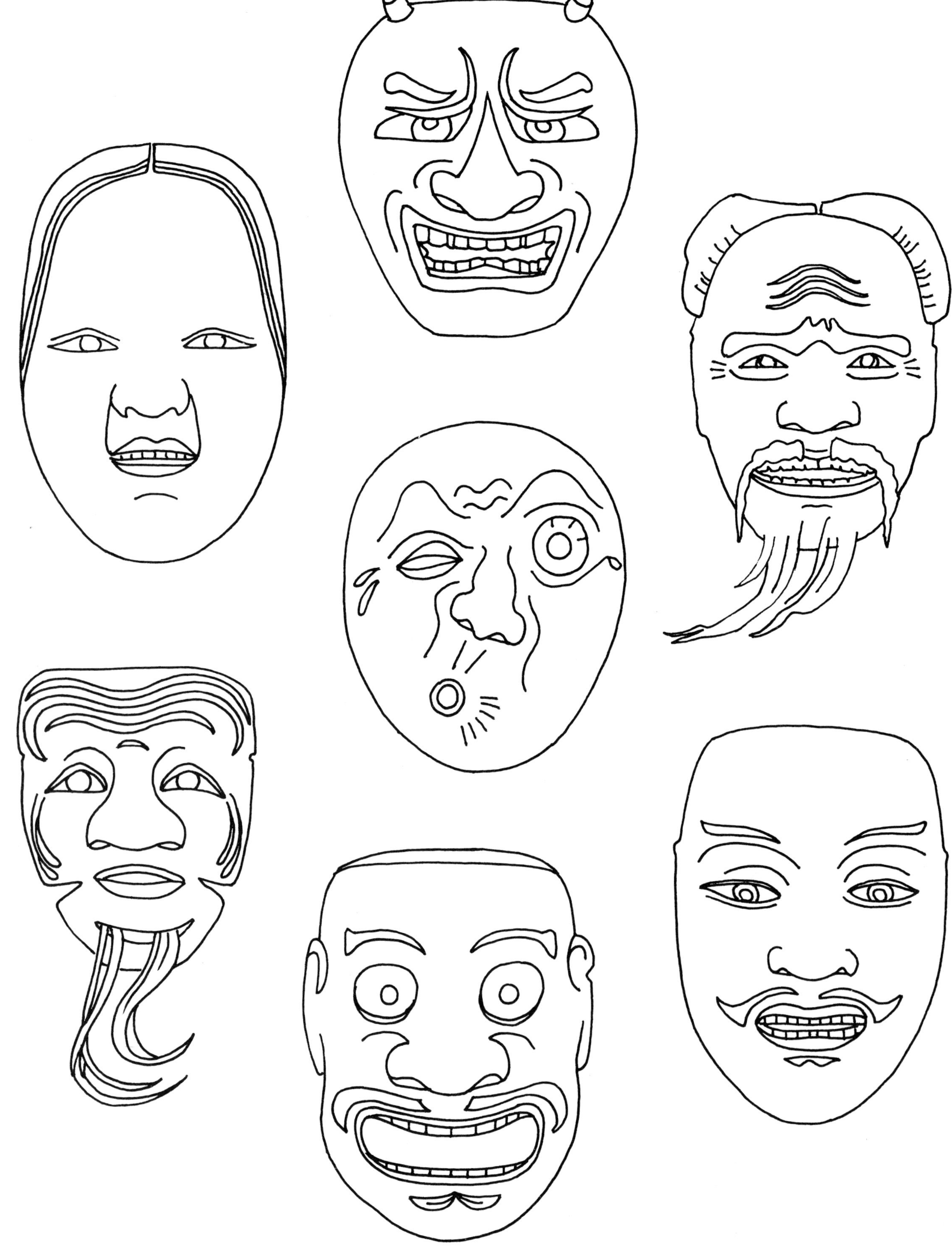

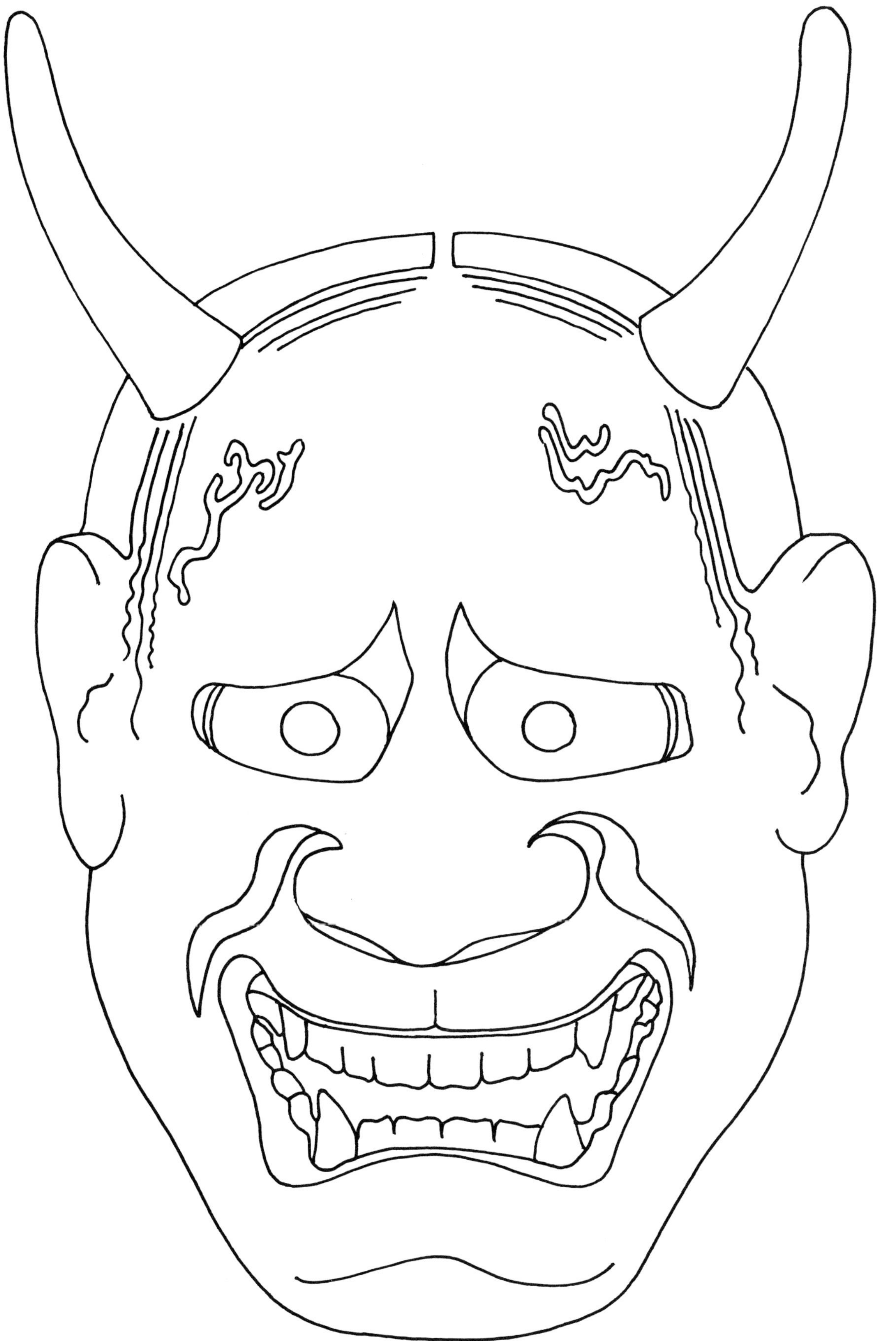

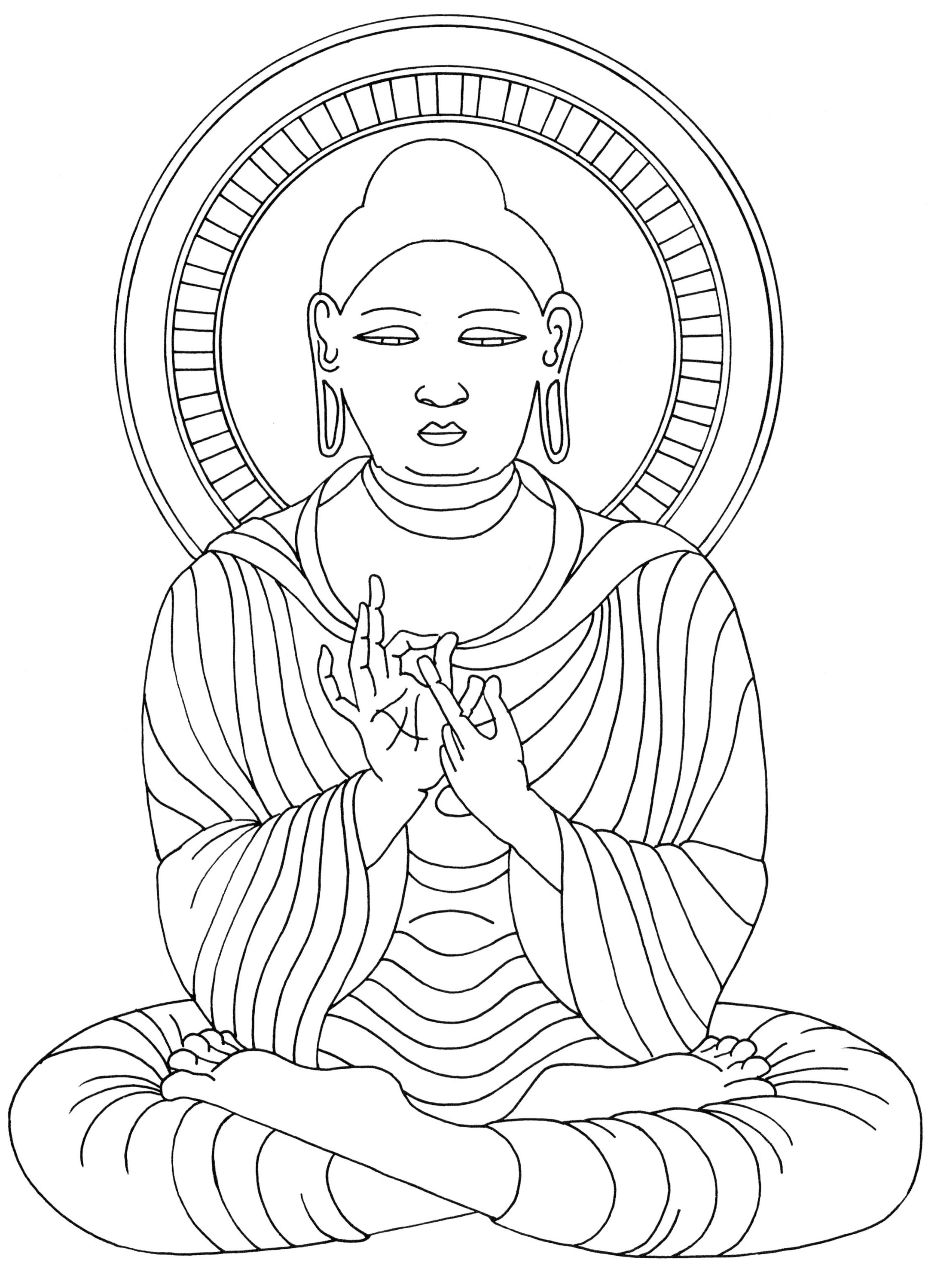

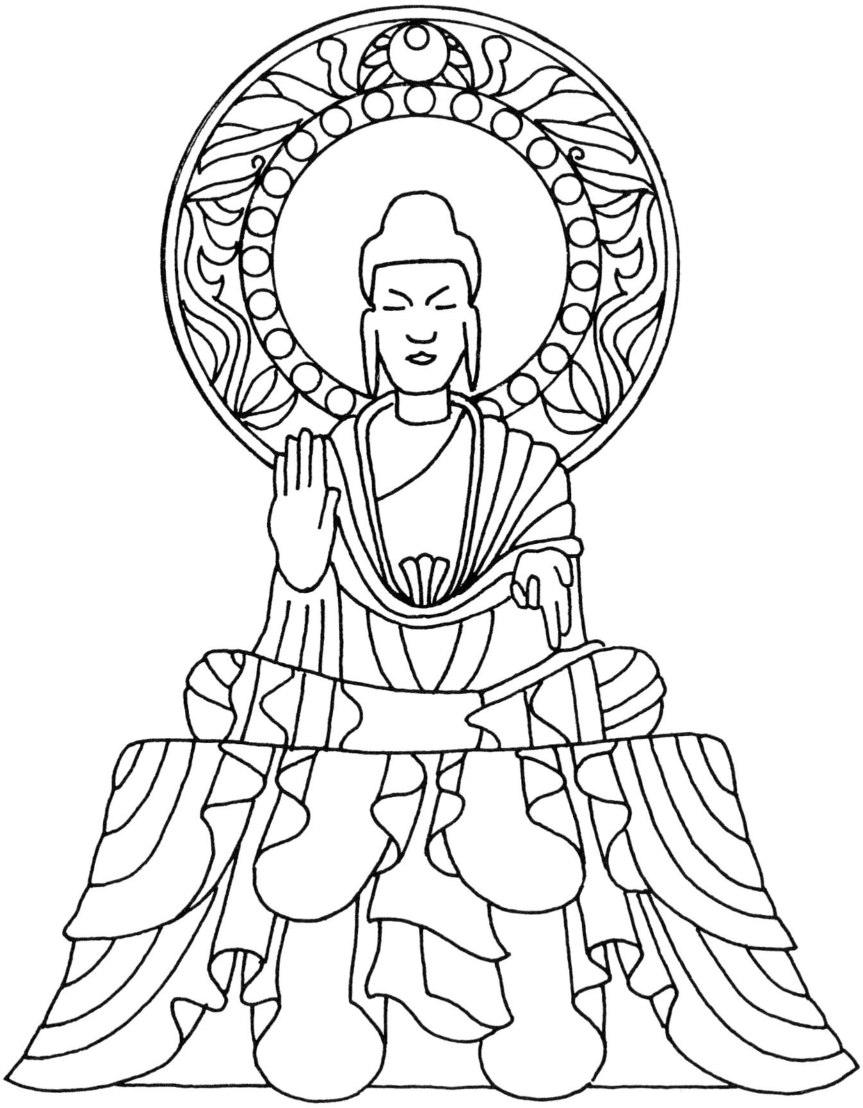

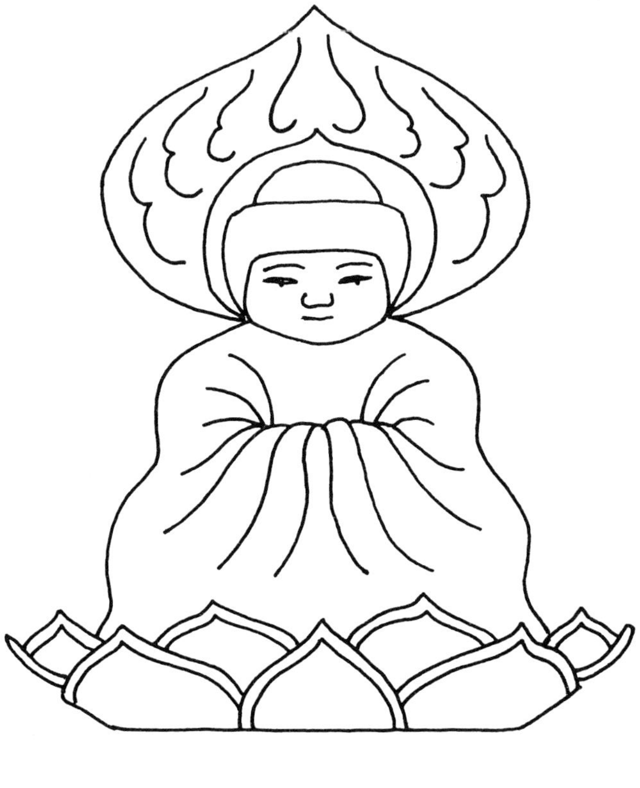

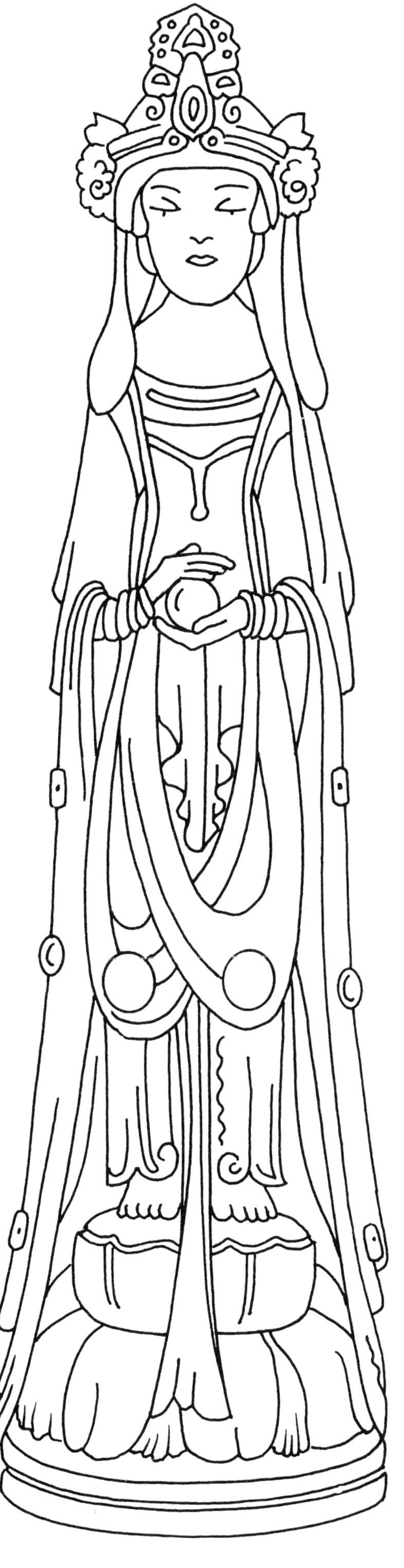

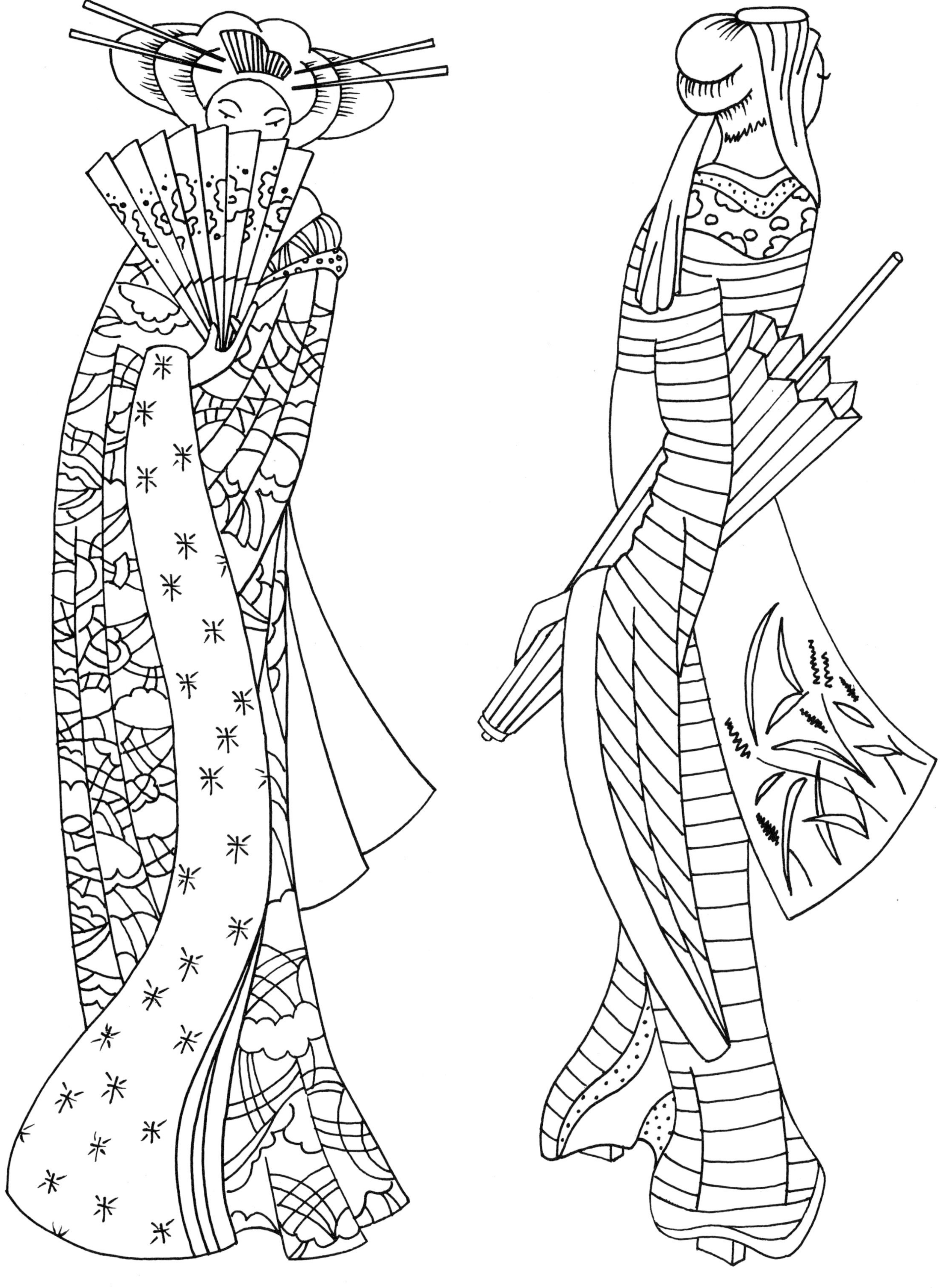